W9-AGK-783

Fix It Quick™

Favorite Brand Name
RECIPES™

Publications International, Ltd.

Favorite Brand Name Recipes at www.fbnr.com

Copyright © 2004 Publications International, Ltd.

All rights reserved. This publication may not be reproduced or quoted in whole or in part by any means whatsoever without written permission from:

Louis Weber, CEO
Publications International, Ltd.
7373 North Cicero Avenue
Lincolnwood, IL 60712

Permission is never granted for commercial purposes.

Favorite Brand Name Recipes and *Fix It Quick* are trademarks of Publications International, Ltd.

All recipes and photographs that contain specific brand names are copyrighted by those companies and/or associations, unless otherwise specified. All photographs *except* those on pages 5, 7, 27, 31, 33, 37, 43, 47, 59, 61, 71, 75, 91, 129, 131, 139, 141, 147, 151, 153, 177 and 181 copyright © Publications International, Ltd.

DOLE® is a registered trademark of Dole Food Company, Inc.

Glad® is a registered trademark of The Glad Products Company.

Kellogg's® and Crispix® are registered trademarks of Kellogg Company.

™/© M&M's, M and the M&M's Characters are trademarks of Mars, Incorporated. © Mars, Inc. 2004.

Carnation, Nestlé, Ortega and Toll House are registered trademarks of Nestlé.

Some of the products listed in this publication may be in limited distribution.

Front cover photography of products by Sanders Studios, Inc.

Pictured on the front cover *(clockwise from top left):* Skillet Sloppy Joe *(page 76)*, Buffalo Chicken Wing Sampler *(page 4)*, Lit'l Smokies 'n' Macaroni 'n' Cheese *(page 100)* and No-Bake Chocolate Peanut Butter Bars *(page 126)*.

Pictured on the back cover *(left to right):* Country French Chicken Skillet *(page 106)*, Salsa Macaroni & Cheese *(page 168)* and Lemony Cheesecake Bars *(page 140)*.

ISBN: 0-7853-9680-2

Library of Congress Control Number: 2003109985

Manufactured in China.

8 7 6 5 4 3 2 1

Microwave Cooking: Microwave ovens vary in wattage. Use the cooking times as guidelines and check for doneness before adding more time.

Preparation/Cooking Times: Preparation times are based on the approximate amount of time required to assemble the recipe before cooking, baking, chilling or serving. These times include preparation steps such as measuring, chopping and mixing. The fact that some preparations and cooking can be done simultaneously is taken into account. Preparation of optional ingredients and serving suggestions is not included.

Contents

Speedy Snacks

Buffalo Chicken Wing Sampler

2½ pounds chicken wing pieces
½ cup *Frank's® RedHot®* Cayenne Pepper Sauce
⅓ cup melted butter

1. Deep-fry* wings in hot oil (400°F) for 12 minutes until fully cooked and crispy; drain.

2. Combine ***Frank's RedHot*** Sauce and butter. Dip wings in sauce to coat.

3. Serve wings with celery and blue cheese dressing if desired.

Makes 8 appetizer servings

*For equally crispy wings, bake 1 hour at 425°F, or grill 30 minutes over medium heat.

RedHot® **Sampler Variations:** Add one of the following to ***RedHot*** butter mixture; heat through. Tex-Mex: 1 tablespoon chili powder; ¼ teaspoon garlic powder. Asian: 2 tablespoons honey, 2 tablespoons teriyaki sauce, 2 teaspoons ground ginger. Sprinkle wings with 1 tablespoon sesame seeds. Zesty Honey-Dijon: Substitute the following blend instead of the ***RedHot*** butter mixture: ¼ cup each ***Frank's® RedHot®*** Sauce, ***French's®*** Napa Valley Style Dijon Mustard and honey.

Prep Time: 5 minutes
Cook Time: 12 minutes

Sweet Pepper Pizza Fingers

2 tablespoons margarine or butter

2 large red, green and/or yellow bell peppers, thinly sliced

1 clove garlic, finely chopped

1 envelope LIPTON® RECIPE SECRETS® Onion Soup Mix

1 cup water

1 package (10 ounces) refrigerated pizza crust

1½ cups shredded mozzarella cheese (about 6 ounces), divided

Preheat oven to 425°F.

In 12-inch skillet, melt margarine over medium heat; cook peppers and garlic, stirring occasionally, 5 minutes or until peppers are tender. Stir in soup mix blended with water. Bring to a boil over high heat. Reduce heat to low and simmer uncovered 6 minutes or until liquid is absorbed. Remove from heat; set aside to cool 5 minutes.

Meanwhile, on baking sheet sprayed with nonstick cooking spray, roll out pizza crust into 12×8-inch rectangle. Sprinkle 1 cup mozzarella cheese over crust; top with cooked pepper mixture, spreading to edges of dough. Top with remaining ½ cup mozzarella cheese. Bake 10 minutes or until crust is golden brown and topping is bubbly. Remove from oven; let stand 5 minutes. To serve, cut into 4×1-inch strips. *Makes about 24 appetizers*

Serving Suggestion: Turn into a main dish by cutting pizza into Sicilian-style square pieces.

Chicken Nachos

22 (about 1 ounce) GUILTLESS GOURMET® Baked Tortilla Chips (yellow, red or blue corn)

½ cup (4 ounces) cooked and shredded boneless chicken breast

¼ cup chopped green onions

¼ cup (1 ounce) grated Cheddar cheese

Sliced green and red chilies (optional)

Microwave Directions

Spread tortilla chips on flat microwave-safe plate. Sprinkle chicken, onions and cheese over chips. Microwave on HIGH 30 seconds until cheese starts to bubble. Serve hot. Garnish with chilies, if desired.

Conventional Directions

Preheat oven to 325°F. Spread tortilla chips on baking sheet. Sprinkle chicken, onions and cheese over chips. Bake about 5 minutes or until cheese starts to bubble. Serve hot.
Makes 22 nachos

Sweet Pepper Pizza Fingers

Hot Artichoke Dip

1 envelope LIPTON® RECIPE SECRETS®
   Onion Soup Mix*

1 can (14 ounces) artichoke hearts,
   drained and chopped

1 cup HELLMANN'S® or BEST FOODS®
   Mayonnaise

1 container (8 ounces) sour cream

1 cup shredded Swiss or mozzarella cheese
   (about 4 ounces)

Also terrific with LIPTON® RECIPE SECRETS® Savory Herb with Garlic, Golden Onion, or Onion-Mushroom Soup Mix.

1. Preheat oven to 350°F. In 1-quart casserole, combine all ingredients.

2. Bake, uncovered, 30 minutes or until heated through.

3. Serve with your favorite dippers.

Makes 3 cups dip

Cold Artichoke Dip: Omit Swiss cheese. Stir in, if desired, ¼ cup grated Parmesan cheese. Do not bake.

Prep Time: 5 minutes
Bake Time: 30 minutes

Quick Tip

When serving hot dip for a party, try baking it in 2 smaller casseroles. When the first casserole is empty, replace it with the second one, fresh from the oven.

Little Turkey Travelers

2 pounds BUTTERBALL® Peppered Turkey
   Breast, sliced thin in the deli

1 jar (16 ounces) mild pepper rings,
   drained

1 can (14 ounces) artichoke hearts,
   drained and quartered

1 jar (8 ounces) mild giardiniera,
   undrained

1 jar (7 ounces) roasted red peppers,
   drained and cut into wide strips

2 packages (8 ounces each) soft cream
   cheese with chives and onion

1 package (17 ounces) soft cracker bread
   (three 16-inch round flat breads)

½ pound thinly sliced provolone cheese

Combine mild peppers, artichoke hearts, giardiniera and roasted peppers in medium bowl. Spread cream cheese on each flat bread. Place turkey and cheese slices on each bread; top each with 1½ cups vegetable mixture.* Roll tightly, jelly-roll style, beginning at the filled end. Wrap each roll in plastic wrap. Chill 2 hours. Cut each roll into 16 slices.

Makes 48 appetizers

For better roll sealing, leave 4 inches across top of each bread covered with cream cheese only.

Prep Time: 30 minutes plus chilling time

Hot Artichoke Dip

Original Ranch® Snack Mix

8 cups KELLOGG'S® CRISPIX® cereal

2½ cups small pretzels

2½ cups bite-size Cheddar cheese crackers (optional)

3 tablespoons vegetable oil

1 packet (1 ounce) HIDDEN VALLEY® The Original Ranch® Salad Dressing & Seasoning Mix

Combine cereal, pretzels and crackers in a gallon-size Glad® Zipper Storage Bag. Pour oil over mixture. Seal bag and toss to coat. Add salad dressing & seasoning mix; seal bag and toss again until coated. *Makes 10 cups*

Original Ranch® Oyster Crackers

1 box (16 ounces) oyster crackers

¼ cup vegetable oil

1 packet (1 ounce) HIDDEN VALLEY® The Original Ranch® Salad Dressing & Seasoning Mix

Place crackers in a gallon size Glad® Fresh Protection Bag. Pour oil over crackers and toss to coat. Add salad dressing mix; toss again until coated. Spread evenly on large baking pan. Bake at 250°F for 15 to 20 minutes.
Makes 8 cups

Ham Spirals

1 (3-ounce) package cream cheese, softened

¼ cup finely chopped dried tart cherries

3 tablespoons finely chopped pecans

2 tablespoons mayonnaise

½ teaspoon honey mustard or spicy brown mustard

4 thin slices cooked ham

Combine cream cheese, dried cherries, pecans, mayonnaise and mustard in small bowl; mix well.

Spread cherry mixture evenly on ham slices. Roll up jelly-roll style; fasten with wooden picks. Let chill several hours. Remove wooden picks. Slice each ham roll crosswise into ¼-inch slices; serve with crackers.
Makes about 40 (¼-inch) pieces

Favorite recipe from **Cherry Marketing Institute**

Quick Tip

Serve snack mixes in small bowls such as wooden salad bowls, cereal bowls or small decorative serving bowls. Place the bowls around the room for easy access to your guests.

Top to bottom: Original Ranch® Snack Mix and Original Ranch® Oyster Crackers

Spicy Cheese 'n' Chili Dip

1 pound BOB EVANS® Special Seasonings Roll Sausage

1 pound pasteurized process cheese spread

1 (10-ounce) can diced tomatoes with green chiles, drained

1 (14- to 16-ounce) bag tortilla chips

Crumble and cook sausage in medium skillet until browned. Drain on paper towels. Combine cheese and tomatoes in medium saucepan; heat until cheese is melted. Stir in sausage. Serve in warm bowl with tortilla chips. *Makes 10 to 12 servings*

Holiday Meatballs

1 package Original or Italian Style Meatballs

1 cup HEINZ® Chili Sauce

1 cup grape jelly

Heat meatballs according to package directions. Meanwhile, in small saucepan, combine chili sauce and grape jelly. Heat until jelly is melted. Place meatballs in serving dish. Pour chili sauce mixture over; stir gently to coat. Serve warm. *Makes 60 appetizers*

Variation: For a zestier sauce, substitute hot jalapeño jelly for grape jelly.

Garlic Onion Bread

½ cup butter or margarine, softened

2 tablespoons minced garlic

1 tablespoon chopped parsley

1 loaf (14 inches) Italian bread, split lengthwise in half

1⅓ cups *French's*® French Fried Onions

¼ cup grated Parmesan cheese

1. Preheat oven to 350°F. Combine butter, garlic and parsley. Spread half the butter mixture onto each cut side of bread. Sprinkle each with
⅔ cup French Fried Onions and 2 tablespoons cheese.

2. Place bread on baking sheet. Bake 5 minutes or until hot and onions are golden brown. Cut each half into 8 slices. *Makes 8 servings*

Variation: You may substitute ⅔ cup prepared pesto sauce for the butter sauce.

Quick Tip

Pesto sauce, a green uncooked sauce usually made from basil, garlic, pine nuts and Parmesan cheese, is excellent to have on hand as a spread for toasted bread or a topping for meats.

BelGioioso Gorgonzola Spread

2 cups BELGIOIOSO® Mascarpone

½ cup BELGIOIOSO® Gorgonzola

2 tablespoons chopped fresh basil

½ cup chopped walnuts

Sliced apples and pears

In small bowl, combine BelGioioso Mascarpone, BelGioioso Gorgonzola and basil. Mix to blend well. Transfer mixture into serving bowl; cover and refrigerate 2 hours. Before serving, sprinkle with walnuts and arrange sliced apples and pears around dish. *Makes 8 servings*

Variation: This spread can also be served with fresh vegetables, crackers, Melba toast or bread.

Sausage Cheese Puffs

1 pound BOB EVANS® Original Recipe Roll Sausage

2½ cups (10 ounces) shredded sharp Cheddar cheese

2 cups biscuit mix

½ cup water

1 teaspoon baking powder

Preheat oven to 350°F. Combine ingredients in large bowl until blended. Shape into 1-inch balls. Place on lightly greased baking sheets. Bake about 25 minutes or until golden brown. Serve hot. Refrigerate leftovers.

Makes about 60 appetizers

Rocky Road Popcorn Balls

6 cups unbuttered popped popcorn, lightly salted

2 cups "M&M's"® Chocolate Mini Baking Bits, divided

1¾ cups peanuts

¼ cup (½ stick) butter

4 cups miniature marshmallows

In large bowl combine popcorn, 1½ cups "M&M's"® Chocolate Mini Baking Bits and peanuts; set aside. Place remaining ½ cup "M&M's"® Chocolate Mini Baking Bits in shallow bowl; set aside. In large saucepan over low heat combine butter and marshmallows until melted, stirring often. Pour marshmallow mixture over popcorn mixture; stir until well coated. Form popcorn mixture into 12 balls; roll in "M&M's"® Chocolate Mini Baking Bits. Store in tightly covered container.

Makes 12 popcorn balls

Quick Tip

Popcorn treats make fun thoughtful gifts. Place individual popcorn balls on cellophane sheets. Gather up the ends and tie together with ribbons.

Green's "Easier Than Pie" Pretzel Sticks

**1 cup "M&M's"® Chocolate Mini
Baking Bits**

**4 squares (1 ounce each) semi-sweet
chocolate, divided**

12 pretzel rods, divided

**4 squares (1 ounce each) white chocolate,
divided**

Line baking sheet with waxed paper; set aside.
Place "M&M's"® Chocolate Mini Baking Bits in
shallow dish; set aside. In top of double boiler
over hot water melt 3 squares semi-sweet
chocolate. Remove from heat. Dip 6 pretzel
rods into chocolate, spooning chocolate to
coat about ¾ of each pretzel. Press into and
sprinkle with "M&M's"® Chocolate Mini Baking
Bits; place on prepared baking sheet.
Refrigerate until chocolate is firm. In top of
double boiler over hot water melt 3 squares
white chocolate. Remove from heat. Dip
remaining 6 pretzel rods into chocolate,
spooning chocolate to coat about ¾ of each
pretzel. Press into and sprinkle with "M&M's"®
Chocolate Mini Baking Bits; place on prepared
baking sheet. Refrigerate until chocolate is
firm. Place remaining 1 square semi-sweet
chocolate in small microwave-safe bowl; place
remaining 1 square white chocolate in
separate small microwave-safe bowl.
Microwave at HIGH 30 seconds; stir. Repeat as
necessary until chocolates are completely
melted, stirring at 10-second intervals. Drizzle
white chocolate over semi-sweet chocolate-
dipped pretzels; drizzle semi-sweet chocolate
over white chocolate-dipped pretzels. Sprinkle
pretzels with any remaining "M&M's"®
Chocolate Mini Baking Bits. Refrigerate
10 minutes or until firm. Store tightly covered
at room temperature.

Makes 12 pretzel sticks

"M&M's"® Family Party Mix

2 tablespoons butter or margarine*

¼ cup honey*

**2 cups favorite grain cereal *or* 3 cups
granola**

1 cup coarsely chopped nuts

1 cup thin pretzel pieces

1 cup raisins

**2 cups "M&M's"® Chocolate Mini
Baking Bits**

**For a drier mix, eliminate butter and honey. Simply
combine dry ingredients and do not bake.*

Preheat oven to 300°F. In large saucepan over
low heat, melt butter; add honey until well
blended. Remove from heat and add cereal,
nuts, pretzel pieces and raisins, stirring until
all pieces are evenly coated. Spread mixture
onto ungreased cookie sheet and bake about
10 minutes. Do not overbake. Spread mixture
onto waxed paper and allow to cool
completely. In large bowl combine mixture
and "M&M's"® Chocolate Mini Baking Bits.
Store in tightly covered container.

Makes about 6 cups snack mix

Green's "Easier Than Pie" Pretzel Sticks

Fresh Garden Dip

1½ cups fat free or reduced fat mayonnaise

1½ cups shredded DOLE® Carrots

1 cup DOLE® Broccoli, finely chopped

⅓ cup finely chopped green onions

2 teaspoons dried dill weed

¼ teaspoon garlic powder

   DOLE® Cauliflower Florets or Peeled
   Mini Carrots

• Stir together mayonnaise, shredded carrots, broccoli, green onions, dill and garlic powder in medium bowl until blended.

• Spoon into serving bowl. Cover and chill 1 hour or overnight. Serve with assorted fresh vegetables. Refrigerate any leftovers in airtight container. *Makes 3½ cups*

Prep Time: 15 minutes
Chill Time: 1 hour

Quick Tip

Keep Garden Dip on hand with prepared vegetables for that spur-of-the-moment snack.

Open-Faced Reubens

1 box (6 ounces) rye melba toast rounds

¼ pound thinly sliced cooked corned beef, cut into ½-inch squares

1 can (8 ounces) sauerkraut, rinsed, drained and chopped

1 cup (4 ounces) finely shredded Wisconsin Swiss cheese

2 teaspoons prepared mustard

   Caraway seeds

Preheat oven to 350°F. Arrange toast rounds on baking sheets. Top each with 1 beef square and 1 teaspoon sauerkraut. Combine cheese and mustard in small bowl; spoon about 1 teaspoon cheese mixture on top of sauerkraut. Sprinkle with caraway seeds. Bake about 5 minutes or until cheese is melted.

Makes about 48 appetizer servings

Microwave Directions: Arrange 8 toast rounds around edge of microwave-safe plate lined with paper towel. Place 2 rounds in center. Top as directed. Microwave, uncovered, on MEDIUM (50% power) 1 to 2 minutes until cheese is melted, turning plate once. Repeat with remaining ingredients.

Favorite recipe from **Wisconsin Milk Marketing Board**

Fresh Garden Dip

Cheese and Pepper Stuffed Potato Skins

6 large russet potatoes (about ¾ pound each), scrubbed

4 tablespoons *Frank's® RedHot®* Cayenne Pepper Sauce, divided

2 tablespoons butter, melted

1 large red bell pepper, seeded and finely chopped

1 cup chopped green onions

1 cup (4 ounces) shredded Cheddar cheese

1. Preheat oven to 450°F. Wrap potatoes in foil; bake about 1 hour 15 minutes or until fork tender. Let stand until cool enough to handle. Cut each potato in half lengthwise; scoop out insides,* leaving a ¼-inch-thick shell. Cut shells in half crosswise. Place shells on large baking sheet.

2. Preheat broiler. Combine 1 tablespoon *Frank's RedHot* Sauce and butter in small bowl; brush on inside of each potato shell. Broil shells, 6 inches from heat, 8 minutes or until golden brown and crispy.

3. Combine remaining 3 tablespoons *Frank's RedHot* Sauce with remaining ingredients in large bowl. Spoon about 1 tablespoon mixture into each potato shell. Broil 2 minutes or until cheese melts. Cut each piece in half to serve.

Makes 12 servings

Reserve leftover potato for mashed potatoes, home-fries or soup.

Prep Time: 30 minutes
Cook Time: 1 hour 20 minutes

Golden Chicken Nuggets

1 envelope LIPTON® RECIPE SECRETS® Golden Onion Soup Mix

½ cup plain dry bread crumbs

1½ pounds boneless, skinless chicken breasts, cut into 2-inch pieces

2 tablespoons margarine or butter, melted

1. Preheat oven to 425°F. In small bowl, combine soup mix and bread crumbs. Dip chicken in bread crumb mixture until evenly coated.

2. On lightly greased cookie sheet, arrange chicken; drizzle with margarine.

3. Bake uncovered 15 minutes or until chicken is thoroughly cooked, turning once.

Makes 6 servings

Variation: Also terrific with Lipton® Recipe Secrets® Onion, Onion Mushroom, or Savory Herb with Garlic Soup Mix.

Prep Time: 10 minutes
Cook Time: 15 minutes

Cheese and Pepper Stuffed Potato Skins

Spinach Dip

1 package (10 ounces) frozen chopped spinach, thawed and squeezed dry

1 container (16 ounces) sour cream

1 cup HELLMANN'S® or BEST FOODS® Mayonnaise

1 package KNORR® Recipe Classics™ Vegetable Soup, Dip and Recipe Mix

1 can (8 ounces) water chestnuts, drained and chopped (optional)

3 green onions, chopped

• In medium bowl, combine all ingredients; chill at least 2 hours to blend flavors.

• Stir before serving. Serve with your favorite dippers.   *Makes about 4 cups dip*

Yogurt Spinach Dip: Substitute 1 container (16 ounces) plain lowfat yogurt for sour cream.

Spinach and Cheese Dip: Add 2 cups (8 ounces) shredded Swiss cheese with spinach.

Prep Time: 10 minutes
Chill Time: 2 hours

Ortega® 7-Layer Dip

1 can (16 ounces) ORTEGA® Refried Beans

1 package (1.25 ounces) ORTEGA® Taco Seasoning Mix

1 container (8 ounces) sour cream

1 container (8 ounces) refrigerated guacamole

1 cup (4 ounces) shredded Cheddar cheese

1 cup ORTEGA® Salsa Prima Homestyle Mild or Thick & Chunky

1 can (4 ounces) ORTEGA® Diced Green Chiles

2 large green onions, sliced

Tortilla chips

COMBINE beans and seasoning mix in small bowl. Spread bean mixture in 8-inch square baking dish.

TOP with sour cream, guacamole, cheese, salsa, chiles and green onions. Serve with chips.   *Makes 10 to 12 servings*

Note: Can be prepared up to 2 hours ahead and refrigerated.

Spinach Dip

Hot 'n' Spicy Italian Stix Mix

6 tablespoons butter or margarine, melted

2 tablespoons *Frank's® RedHot®* Cayenne Pepper Sauce

1 tablespoon *French's®* Worcestershire Sauce

4 cups oven-toasted rice cereal squares

2⅔ cups *French's®* French Fried Onions, divided

2 cans (1½ ounces each) *French's®* Potato Sticks

¼ cup grated Parmesan cheese

1 package (1.25 ounces) Italian spaghetti sauce mix

1. Preheat oven to 250°F. Combine butter, ***Frank's RedHot*** Sauce and Worcestershire in glass measuring cup. Place remaining ingredients in shallow roasting pan; mix well. Pour butter mixture over cereal mixture; toss to coat evenly.

2. Bake 30 minutes or until crispy, stirring twice. Cool completely. *Makes 7 cups mix*

Prep Time: 15 minutes
Cook Time: 30 minutes

BLT Dip

1 envelope LIPTON® RECIPE SECRETS® Onion Soup Mix*

1 container (8 ounces) sour cream

1 cup HELLMANN'S® or BEST FOODS® Mayonnaise

1 medium tomato, chopped (about 1 cup)

½ cup cooked crumbled bacon (about 6 slices) or bacon bits

Shredded lettuce

*Also terrific with LIPTON® RECIPE SECRETS® Golden Onion Soup Mix.

1. In medium bowl, combine all ingredients except lettuce; chill if desired.

2. Garnish with lettuce and serve with your favorite dippers. *Makes 3 cups dip*

Prep Time: 10 minutes

Quick Tip

For easy entertaining, serve dips with a creative variety of dippers. Keep assorted crackers, bagel or pita chips on hand for last minute snacks. Use mozzarella sticks, cooked tortellini and cherry tomatoes for other interesting dippers.

Buffalo-Style Chicken Nachos

2 cups diced cooked chicken

⅓ cup *Frank's® RedHot®* Cayenne Pepper Sauce

2 tablespoons melted butter

1 bag (10 ounces) tortilla chips

3 cups shredded Cheddar or Monterey Jack cheese

1. Preheat oven to 350°F. Combine chicken, *Frank's RedHot* Sauce and butter. Layer chips, chicken and cheese in ovenproof serving dish or baking dish.

2. Bake 5 minutes just until cheese melts. Garnish as desired. Splash on more *Frank's RedHot* Sauce to taste.   *Makes 4 servings*

Prep Time: 5 minutes
Cook Time: 5 minutes

Rock Pop Trail Mix

1 (3-ounce) bag ORVILLE REDENBACHER'S® Microwave Popping Corn, popped according to package directions

1 cup dried fruit, diced

½ cup raisins

½ cup reduced fat honey roasted nuts

2 tablespoons powdered sugar

1 teaspoon ground cinnamon

1. Place Orville Redenbacher's Popcorn in large bowl.

2. Toss in fruit, raisins and nuts.

3. Combine sugar and cinnamon; sift over popcorn mixture.
Makes 13 (1-cup) servings

Quick Tip

Divide Trail Mix into individual servings and store in small resealable plastic food storage bags for on-the-go snacks.

Effortless Brunches

Cinnamon Chip Filled Crescents

2 cans (8 ounces each) refrigerated quick crescent dinner rolls
2 tablespoons butter or margarine, melted
1⅔ cups (10-ounce package) HERSHEY'S Cinnamon Chips, divided
  Cinnamon Chips Drizzle (recipe follows)

1. Heat oven to 375°F. Unroll dough; separate into 16 triangles.

2. Spread melted butter on each triangle. Sprinkle 1 cup cinnamon chips evenly over triangles; gently press chips into dough. Roll from shortest side of triangle to opposite point. Place, point side down, on ungreased cookie sheet; curve into crescent shape.

3. Bake 8 to 10 minutes or until golden brown. Drizzle with Cinnamon Drizzle. Serve warm.   *Makes 16 crescents*

Cinnamon Chips Drizzle: Place remaining ⅔ cup chips and 1½ teaspoons shortening (do not use butter, margarine, spread or oil) in small microwave-safe bowl. Microwave at HIGH (100%) 1 minute; stir until chips are melted.

Blueberry Orange Muffins

1 package DUNCAN HINES® Bakery-Style Wild Maine Blueberry Muffin Mix

½ **cup orange juice**

2 egg whites

1 teaspoon grated orange peel

1. Preheat oven to 400°F. Grease 2½-inch muffin cups (or use paper liners).

2. Rinse blueberries from Mix with cold water and drain.

3. Empty muffin mix into large bowl. Break up any lumps. Add orange juice, egg whites and orange peel. Stir until moistened, about 50 strokes. Fold blueberries gently into batter.

4. For large muffins, fill cups two-thirds full. Bake at 400°F for 18 to 21 minutes or until toothpick inserted into centers comes out clean. (For medium muffins, fill cups half full. Bake at 400°F for 16 to 19 minutes or until toothpick inserted into centers comes out clean.) Cool in pan 5 to 10 minutes. Carefully loosen muffins from pan. Remove to cooling racks. Serve warm or cool completely.

Makes 8 large or 12 medium muffins

Quick Tip

Freeze extra grated orange peel for future use.

Berry Filled Muffins

1 package DUNCAN HINES® Bakery-Style Wild Maine Blueberry Muffin Mix

1 egg

½ **cup water**

¼ **cup strawberry jam**

2 tablespoons sliced natural almonds

1. Preheat oven to 400°F. Place 8 (2½-inch) paper or foil liners in muffin cups; set aside.

2. Rinse blueberries from Mix with cold water and drain.

3. Empty muffin mix into bowl. Break up any lumps. Add egg and water. Stir until moistened, about 50 strokes. Fill cups half full with batter.

4. Fold blueberries into jam. Spoon on top of batter in each cup. Spread gently. Cover with remaining batter. Sprinkle with almonds. Bake at 400°F for 17 to 20 minutes or until set and golden brown. Cool in pan 5 to 10 minutes. Loosen carefully before removing from pan.

Makes 8 muffins

Variation: For a delicious flavor variation, try using blackberry or red raspberry jam instead of the strawberry jam.

Blueberry Orange Muffins

Whip 'em Up Wacky Waffles

1½ cups biscuit baking mix

1 cup buttermilk

1 large egg

1 tablespoon vegetable oil

½ cup "M&M's"® Semi-Sweet Chocolate Mini Baking Bits

Powdered sugar and maple syrup

Preheat Belgian waffle iron. In large bowl combine baking mix, buttermilk, egg and oil until well mixed. Spoon about ½ cup batter into hot waffle iron. Sprinkle with about 2 tablespoons "M&M's"® Semi-Sweet Chocolate Mini Baking Bits; top with about ½ cup batter. Close lid and bake until steaming stops, 1 to 2 minutes.* Sprinkle with powdered sugar and serve immediately with maple syrup and additional "M&M's"® Semi-Sweet Chocolate Mini Baking Bits.

Makes 4 Belgian waffles

*Check the manufacturer's directions for recommended amount of batter and baking time.

Chocolate Waffles: Substitute 1¼ cups biscuit baking mix, ¼ cup unsweetened cocoa powder and ½ cup sugar for biscuit baking mix above. Prepare and cook as directed above.

Quick Tip

These waffles make a great dessert too! Serve them with a scoop of ice cream, chocolate sauce and a sprinkle of "M&M's"® Chocolate Mini Baking Bits.

Hearty Banana Carrot Muffins

2 ripe, medium DOLE® Bananas

1 package (14 ounces) oat bran muffin mix

¾ teaspoon ground ginger

1 medium DOLE® Carrot, shredded (½ cup)

⅓ cup light molasses

⅓ cup DOLE® Seedless or Golden Raisins

¼ cup chopped almonds

• Mash bananas with fork (1 cup).

• Combine muffin mix and ginger in large bowl. Add carrot, molasses, raisins and bananas. Stir just until moistened.

• Spoon batter into paper-lined muffin cups. Sprinkle tops with almonds.

• Bake at 425°F 12 to 14 minutes until browned.

Makes 12 muffins

Prep Time: 20 minutes
Bake Time: 14 minutes

Coconut Chocolate Chip Loaf

1 package DUNCAN HINES® Bakery-Style Chocolate Chip Muffin Mix

1⅓ cups toasted flaked coconut (see Quick Tip)

¾ cup water

1 egg

½ teaspoon vanilla extract

Confectioners' sugar for garnish (optional)

1. Preheat oven to 350°F. Grease and flour 9×5×3-inch loaf pan.

2. Empty muffin mix into medium bowl. Break up any lumps. Add coconut, water, egg and vanilla extract. Stir until moistened, about 50 strokes. Pour into prepared pan. Bake at 350°F for 45 to 50 minutes or until toothpick inserted in center comes out clean. Cool in pan 15 minutes. Invert onto cooling rack. Turn right side up. Cool completely. Dust with confectioners' sugar, if desired.

Makes 1 loaf (12 slices)

Quick Tip

To toast coconut in the oven, spread evenly on a baking sheet. Toast at 350°F for 5 minutes. Stir and toast 1 to 2 minutes longer or until light golden brown. To toast coconut in the microwave, evenly spread coconut on a microwavable plate. Heat at HIGH (100% power) 4 to 5 minutes or just until golden. Stir coconut after each minute to ensure even toasting.

Breakfast Blossoms

1 (12-ounce) can buttermilk biscuits (10 biscuits)

¾ cup SMUCKER'S® Strawberry Preserves

¼ teaspoon ground cinnamon

¼ teaspoon ground nutmeg

Grease ten 2½- or 3-inch muffin cups. Separate dough into 10 biscuits. Separate each biscuit into 3 even sections or leaves. Stand 3 sections evenly around side and bottom of cup, overlapping slightly. Press dough edges firmly together.

Combine preserves, cinnamon and nutmeg; place tablespoonful in center of each cup.

Bake at 375°F for 10 to 12 minutes or until lightly browned. Cool slightly before removing from pan. Serve warm.   *Makes 10 rolls*

Quick Tip

Make bite-size Breakfast Blossoms using miniature muffin pans. Carefully press one section of a biscuit in each muffin cup. Fill with 1 teaspoon of filling. Bake as directed above.

Coconut Chocolate Chip Loaf

Peachy Cinnamon Coffeecake

1 can (8¼ ounces) juice packed sliced yellow cling peaches
1 package DUNCAN HINES® Bakery-Style Cinnamon Swirl Muffin Mix
1 egg

1. Preheat oven to 400°F. Grease 8-inch square or 9-inch round pan.

2. Drain peaches, reserving juice. Add water to reserved juice to equal ¾ cup liquid. Chop peaches.

3. Combine muffin mix, egg and ¾ cup peach liquid in medium bowl; fold in peaches. Pour batter into prepared pan. Knead swirl packet 10 seconds before opening. Squeeze contents onto top of batter and swirl with knife. Sprinkle topping over batter. Bake at 400°F for 28 to 33 minutes for 8-inch pan (or 20 to 25 minutes for 9-inch pan) or until golden. Serve warm. *Makes 9 servings*

Cranberry Pecan Muffins

1½ cups fresh or frozen cranberries
¼ cup light corn syrup
1 package DUNCAN HINES® Bakery-Style Cinnamon Swirl Muffin Mix
1 egg
¾ cup water or milk
½ cup chopped pecans

1. Preheat oven to 400°F. Place 14 (2½-inch) paper liners in muffin cups. Place cranberries and corn syrup in heavy saucepan. Cook on medium heat, stirring occasionally, until cranberries pop and mixture is slightly thickened. Drain cranberries in strainer; set aside.

2. Empty muffin mix into medium bowl. Break up any lumps. Add egg and water. Stir until moistened, about 50 strokes. Stir in cranberries and pecans. Knead swirl packet from Mix for 10 seconds before opening. Cut off 1 end of swirl packet. Squeeze contents over top of batter. Swirl into batter with knife or spatula. *Do not completely mix in.* Spoon batter into muffin cups (see Tip). Sprinkle with contents of topping packet from Mix. Bake at 400°F for 18 to 22 minutes or until toothpick inserted into centers comes out clean. Cool in pans 5 to 10 minutes. Serve warm or cool completely. *Makes 14 muffins*

Tip: Fill an equal number of muffin cups in each muffin pan with batter. For more even baking, fill empty muffin cups with ½ inch of water.

Peachy Cinnamon Coffeecake

Blueberry White Chip Muffins

2 cups all-purpose flour

½ cup granulated sugar

¼ cup packed brown sugar

2½ teaspoons baking powder

½ teaspoon salt

¾ cup milk

1 large egg, slightly beaten

¼ cup butter or margarine, melted

½ teaspoon grated lemon peel

2 cups (12-ounce package) NESTLE® TOLLHOUSE® Premier White Morsels, *divided*

Streusel Topping (recipe follows)

PREHEAT oven to 375°F. Paper-line 18 muffin cups.

COMBINE flour, granulated sugar, brown sugar, baking powder and salt in large bowl. Stir in milk, egg, butter and lemon peel. Stir in *1½ cups* morsels and blueberries. Spoon into prepared muffin cups, filling almost full. Sprinkle with Streusel Topping.

BAKE for 22 to 25 minutes or until wooden pick inserted into center comes out clean. Cool in pans for 5 minutes; remove to wire racks to cool slightly.

PLACE *remaining* morsels in small, *heavy-duty* resealable plastic food storage bag. Microwave on MEDIUM-HIGH (70%) power for 30 seconds; knead. Microwave at additional 10- to 20-second intervals, kneading until smooth. Cut tiny corner from bag; squeeze to drizzle over muffins.   *Makes 18 muffins*

Streusel Topping: **COMBINE** ⅓ cup granulated sugar, ¼ cup all-purpose flour and ¼ teaspoon ground cinnamon in small bowl. Cut in 3 tablespoons butter or margarine with pastry blender or two knives until mixture resembles coarse crumbs.

Butterscotch Crescents

½ cup HERSHEY'S Butterscotch Chips

¼ cup MOUNDS® Sweetened Coconut Flakes

2 tablespoons finely chopped nuts

1 can (8 ounces) refrigerated quick crescent dinner rolls

Powdered sugar

1. Heat oven to 375°F.

2. Stir together butterscotch chips, coconut and nuts in small bowl. Unroll crescent roll dough to form eight triangles. Lightly sprinkle 1 heaping tablespoon butterscotch mixture on top of each; gently press into dough. Starting at short side of each triangle, roll dough to opposite point. Place rolls, point side down, on ungreased cookie sheet; curve into crescent shapes.

3. Bake 10 to 12 minutes or until golden brown. Sprinkle with powdered sugar. Serve warm.   *Makes 8 crescents*

Blueberry White Chip Muffins

Spring Break Blueberry Coffeecake

Topping

½ cup flaked coconut

¼ cup firmly packed brown sugar

2 tablespoons butter or margarine, softened

1 tablespoon all-purpose flour

Cake

1 package DUNCAN HINES® Bakery-Style Wild Maine Blueberry Muffin Mix

1 can (8 ounces) crushed pineapple with juice, undrained

1 egg

¼ cup water

1. Preheat oven to 350°F. Grease 9-inch square pan.

2. For topping, combine coconut, brown sugar, butter and flour in small bowl. Mix with fork until well blended. Set aside.

3. Rinse blueberries from Mix with cold water and drain.

4. For cake, place muffin mix in medium bowl. Break up any lumps. Add pineapple with juice, egg and water. Stir until moistened, about 50 strokes. Fold in blueberries. Spread in pan. Sprinkle reserved topping over batter. Bake at 350°F for 30 to 35 minutes or until toothpick inserted into center comes out clean. Serve warm, or cool completely.

Makes 9 servings

Huevos Rancheros Tostados

1 can (8 ounces) tomato sauce

⅓ cup prepared salsa or picante sauce

¼ cup chopped fresh cilantro or thinly sliced green onions

4 large eggs

Butter or margarine

4 (6-inch) corn tortillas, crisply fried or 4 prepared tostada shells

1 cup (4 ounces) SARGENTO® Taco Blend Shredded Cheese

Combine tomato sauce, salsa and cilantro; heat in microwave oven or in saucepan over medium-high heat until hot. Fry eggs in butter, sunny side up. Place one egg on each tortilla; top with sauce. Sprinkle with cheese.

Makes 4 servings

Variation: Spread tortillas with heated refried beans before topping with eggs, if desired.

Quick Tip

To keep blueberries from discoloring the batter of coffeecake, drain them on paper towels after rinsing.

Spring Break Blueberry Coffeecake

Spinach & Egg Casserole

1 box (10 ounces) BIRDS EYE® frozen Chopped Spinach

1 can (15 ounces) Cheddar cheese soup

1 tablespoon mustard

½ pound deli ham, cut into ¼-inch cubes

4 hard-boiled eggs, chopped or sliced

- Preheat oven to 350°F.

- In large saucepan, cook spinach according to package directions; drain well.

- Stir in soup, mustard and ham.

- Pour into 9×9-inch baking pan. Top with eggs.

- Bake 15 to 20 minutes or until heated through. *Makes 4 servings*

Prep Time: 10 minutes
Cook Time: 15 to 20 minutes

Huevos Rancheros

1 cup GUILTLESS GOURMET® Salsa (Roasted Red Pepper or Southwestern Grill)

2 eggs

2 corn tortillas (6 inches each)

2 tablespoons low fat sour cream

1 tablespoon chopped fresh cilantro

Bring salsa to a boil in small nonstick skillet over medium heat. Gently break eggs into salsa, being careful not to break yolks. Reduce heat to medium-low; cover and simmer 5 minutes or to desired firmness.

Meanwhile, to soften tortillas, wrap in damp paper towel. Microwave on HIGH (100%) 20 seconds. Or, to soften tortillas in oven, preheat oven to 300°F. Wrap tortillas in foil. Bake 10 minutes. To serve, arrange 1 tortilla on serving plate; top with 1 egg and half the salsa. Dollop with 1 tablespoon sour cream and sprinkle with ½ tablespoon cilantro. Repeat with remaining ingredients.

Makes 2 servings

Golden Apple Oatmeal

½ cup diced Washington Golden Delicious apple

⅓ cup apple juice

⅓ cup water

¼ teaspoon salt (optional)

⅛ teaspoon ground cinnamon

⅛ teaspoon ground nutmeg

⅓ cup uncooked quick-cooking rolled oats

In small pot, combine apple, juice, water, salt, if desired, cinnamon, and nutmeg; heat to a boil. Stir in oats and cook 1 minute. Cover and let stand 2 minutes before serving.

Makes 2 (½-cup) servings

Favorite recipe from **Washington Apple Commission**

Spinach & Egg Casserole

Spanish Omelet

8 large eggs, beaten

3 cups (16 ounces) frozen cubed or
  shredded hash brown potatoes

1½ cups *French's*® French Fried Onions

Salsa

Frank's® RedHot® Cayenne Pepper Sauce

1. Beat eggs with ½ *teaspoon salt* and
¼ *teaspoon pepper* in large bowl; set aside.

2. Heat *2 tablespoons oil* until very hot in
10-inch nonstick oven-safe skillet over
medium-high heat. Sauté potatoes about
7 minutes or until browned, stirring often.

3. Stir ½ *cup* French Fried Onions and beaten
eggs into potato mixture. Cook, uncovered,
over low heat 15 minutes or until eggs are
almost set. *Do not stir.* Sprinkle eggs with
remaining *1 cup* onions. Cover and cook
8 minutes or until eggs are fully set. Cut into
wedges and serve with salsa. Splash on *Frank's
RedHot* Sauce to taste.   *Makes 6 servings*

Prep Time: 5 minutes
Cook Time: 30 minutes

Mexican Frittata

3 tablespoons butter or margarine

2 cups (8 ounces) frozen ready-to-cook
  hash brown potatoes with peppers
  and onions (O'Brien style), thawed*

5 eggs

½ cup salsa

¼ teaspoon salt

2 cups (8 ounces) SARGENTO® Mexican
  Blend Shredded Cheese, divided

Sour cream (optional)

Chopped fresh cilantro (optional)

*To thaw frozen potatoes, microwave at HIGH 2 to
3 minutes.*

Melt butter in 10-inch ovenproof skillet over
high heat. Swirl butter up side of pan to
prevent frittata from sticking. Add potatoes
to skillet; cook 3 minutes, stirring occasionally.
Reduce heat to medium.

Beat eggs in medium bowl. Stir in salsa and
salt. Stir in 1 cup of cheese. Add egg mixture
to skillet; stir gently to combine. Cover; cook
6 minutes without stirring or until eggs are set
around edges. (Center will be wet.) Sprinkle
remaining 1 cup cheese evenly over frittata.
Place under preheated broiler 4 to 5 inches
from heat source. Broil 2 to 3 minutes or until
cheese is melted and eggs are set in center. Cut
into wedges; serve with sour cream and
cilantro, if desired.   *Makes 4 servings*

Spanish Omelet

Effortless Brunches

Brunch Sandwiches

4 English muffins, split, lightly toasted

8 thin slices CURE 81® ham

8 teaspoons Dijon mustard

8 large eggs, fried or poached

8 slices SARGENTO® Deli Style Sliced Swiss Cheese

Top each muffin half with a slice of ham, folding to fit. Spread mustard lightly over ham; top with an egg and one slice cheese. Transfer to foil-lined baking sheet. Broil 4 to 5 inches from heat source until cheese is melted and sandwiches are hot, 2 to 3 minutes.

Makes 4 servings

Maple Apple Oatmeal

2 cups apple juice

1½ cups water

⅓ cup AUNT JEMIMA® Syrup

½ teaspoon ground cinnamon

¼ teaspoon salt (optional)

2 cups QUAKER® Oats (quick or old fashioned, uncooked)

1 cup chopped fresh unpeeled apple

In a 3-quart saucepan, bring juice, water, syrup, cinnamon and salt, if desired, to a boil. Stir in oats and apple. Return to a boil; reduce heat to medium-low. Cook about 1 minute for quick oats (or 5 minutes for old fashioned oats) or until most of liquid is absorbed, stirring occasionally. Let stand until of desired consistency.

Makes 4 servings

Lit'l Links Soufflé

8 slices white bread

2 cups (8 ounces) shredded Cheddar cheese

1 pound HILLSHIRE FARM® Lit'l Polskas

6 eggs

2¾ cups milk

¾ teaspoon dry mustard

Spread bread in bottom of greased 13×9-inch baking pan. Sprinkle cheese over top of bread.

Arrange Lit'l Polskas on top of cheese. Beat eggs with milk and mustard in large bowl; pour over links. Cover pan with aluminum foil; refrigerate overnight.

Preheat oven to 300°F. Bake egg mixture 1½ hours or until puffy and brown.

Makes 4 to 6 servings

Quick Tip

For a fantastic meal to start your weekend, serve breakfast egg dishes such as soufflés, fritattas and omelets with a bowl of cut-up fresh fruit and your best hot coffee or tea.

Cheddar Broccoli Tart

1½ cups milk

3 eggs

1 package KNORR® Recipe Classics™ Leek Soup, Dip and Recipe Mix

1 package (10 ounces) frozen chopped broccoli, thawed and drained

1½ cups shredded Cheddar, Swiss or Monterey Jack cheese (about 6 ounces)

1 (9-inch) unbaked or frozen deep-dish pie crust*

*If using 9-inch deep-dish frozen prepared pie crust, do not thaw. Preheat oven and cookie sheet. Pour filling into pie crust; bake on cookie sheet.

• Preheat oven to 375°F. In large bowl, with fork, beat milk, eggs and recipe mix until blended. Stir in broccoli and cheese; spoon into pie crust.

• Bake 40 minutes or until knife inserted 1 inch from edge comes out clean. Let stand 10 minutes before serving.

Makes 6 servings

Serving Suggestion: Cheddar Broccoli Tart is perfect for brunch or lunch. Or serve it with a mixed green salad and soup for a hearty dinner.

Prep Time: 10 minutes
Cook Time: 40 minutes

Down-Home Sausage Gravy

1 package (16 ounces) fresh breakfast sausage

2 tablespoons finely chopped onion

6 tablespoons all-purpose flour

2 cans (12 fluid ounces *each*) NESTLÉ® CARNATION® Evaporated Milk

1 cup water

¼ teaspoon salt

Hot pepper sauce to taste

Hot biscuits

COMBINE sausage and onion in large skillet. Cook over medium-low heat, stirring occasionally, until sausage is no longer pink. Stir in flour; mix well. Stir in evaporated milk, water, salt and hot pepper sauce. Cook, stirring occasionally, until mixture comes to a boil. Cook for 1 to 2 minutes.

SERVE immediately over biscuits.

Makes 8 to 10 servings

Quick Tip

Unopened packages of sausage can be stored in the freezer for up to 2 months. Keep a package of sausage on hand for spur-of-the-moment brunches.

Cheddar Broccoli Tart

Tacos de Huevos

10 eggs, beaten

½ cup salsa

¼ cup chopped green onions

½ teaspoon LAWRY'S® Seasoned Salt

2 tablespoons butter or margarine

1 package (10 count) LAWRY'S® Taco Shells

3 medium tomatoes, chopped

   Shredded lettuce

1 cup (4 ounces) shredded cheddar cheese

In large bowl, combine eggs, ½ cup salsa, green onions and Seasoned Salt; mix well. In large nonstick skillet, heat butter. Add eggs and scramble eggs over medium heat to desired doneness. Meanwhile, heat Taco Shells in 350°F oven 5 minutes. When eggs are cooked, spoon equal amounts into each Taco Shell. Top with tomatoes, lettuce and cheese. Serve immediately. *Makes 10 tacos*

Serving Suggestion: Serve with salsa and fresh fruit.

Hint: Double the recipe for a larger fiesta!

Leek Frittata

6 eggs

¾ cup milk

1 package KNORR® Recipe Classics™ Leek Soup, Dip and Recipe Mix

1 tablespoon vegetable oil

½ cup shredded Cheddar cheese (2 ounces)

• In medium bowl, with wire whisk, beat eggs and milk until smooth; stir in recipe mix.

• In large nonstick skillet, heat oil over medium heat. Add egg mixture and immediately reduce heat to low. Cover and cook 3 minutes.

• Uncover, stir well and sprinkle with cheese. Cover and cook 3 minutes longer. Let stand covered 5 minutes. *Makes 3 to 4 servings*

Prep Time: 15 minutes

Quick Tip

A frittata is an Italian omelet. The ingredients are mixed into the egg mixture and slowly cooked, often in the oven.

Tacos de Huevos

Fruit 'n Juice Breakfast Shake

1 extra-ripe, medium DOLE® Banana

¾ cup DOLE® Pineapple Juice

½ cup lowfat vanilla yogurt

½ cup blueberries

Combine all ingredients in blender. Process until smooth. *Makes 2 servings*

Orange-Pineapple Breakfast Shake with Yogurt and Honey

1 cup orange or tangerine juice

½ cup unsweetened pineapple juice

½ cup plain low fat yogurt

1 teaspoon honey

Orange twists or fresh mint leaves for garnish (optional)

Add orange juice, pineapple juice, yogurt and honey to food processor or blender. Process until smooth. Pour into two glasses. Garnish with orange twists or fresh mint sprigs, if desired. Serve immediately.

Makes 2 servings

Favorite recipe from **Florida Department of Citrus**

Hot Merry Mocha

6 tablespoons HERSHEY'S Cocoa

1 to 2 tablespoons powdered instant coffee

⅛ teaspoon salt

6 cups hot water

1 can (14 ounces) sweetened condensed milk

Sweetened whipped cream (optional)

1. Stir together cocoa, instant coffee and salt in 4-quart saucepan; stir in water. Cook over medium heat, stirring occasionally, until mixture boils.

2. Stir in sweetened condensed milk. Heat thoroughly; do not boil. Beat with rotary beater or wire whisk until foamy. Serve hot, topped with sweetened whipped cream, if desired. *Makes about 10 (6-ounce) servings*

Minted Hot Chocolate: Follow directions above omitting instant coffee. Stir in ¼ to ½ teaspoon mint extract before beating. Serve with candy cane for stirrer, if desired.

Quick Tip

To make a delicious summer chocolate beverage, Icy Merry Mocha, chill this recipe. Omit the whipped cream and serve over ice.

Peanut Butter Breakfast Shake

1 cup fat free milk

1 banana, peeled and sliced

¼ cup PETER PAN® Smart Choice Creamy Peanut Butter

1 tablespoon honey

1 teaspoon vanilla

2 cups ice cubes

1. In blender, combine *all* ingredients *except* ice. Blend for 5 seconds to mix well.

2. Add ice and continue blending until ice is finely blended and mixture is slushy.

Makes 4 (6-ounce) servings

Pineberry Smoothie

1 ripe DOLE® Banana, quartered

1 cup DOLE® Pineapple Juice

½ cup nonfat vanilla or plain yogurt

½ cup fresh or frozen strawberries, raspberries or blueberries

Combine all ingredients in blender or food processor container. Blend until thick and smooth. Serve immediately.

Makes 2 servings

Prep Time: 5 minutes

Light and Steamy Hot Cocoa

3 tablespoons sugar

2 tablespoons HERSHEY'S Cocoa

¼ cup hot water

1½ cups nonfat milk

⅛ teaspoon vanilla extract

Stir together sugar and cocoa in small saucepan; gradually stir in water. Cook over medium heat, stirring constantly, until mixture boils; boil and stir 2 minutes. Immediately stir in milk; continue cooking and stirring until mixture is hot. *Do not boil.* Remove from heat; stir in vanilla. Serve immediately.

Makes 2 (7-ounce) servings

Quick Tip

For an extra special treat, serve cocoa with cinnamon or peppermint sticks as stirrers.

Lunch Express

Rapid Ragú® Chili

1½ **pounds lean ground beef**
1 **medium onion, chopped**
2 **tablespoons chili powder**
1 **can (19 ounces) red kidney beans, rinsed and drained**
1 **jar (1 pound 10 ounces) RAGÚ® Old World Style® Pasta Sauce**
1 **cup shredded Cheddar cheese (about 4 ounces)**

1. In 12-inch skillet, brown ground beef with onion and chili powder over medium-high heat, stirring occasionally. Stir in beans and Ragú Pasta Sauce.

2. Bring to a boil over high heat. Reduce heat to low and simmer covered, stirring occasionally, 20 minutes. Top with cheese. Serve, if desired, over hot cooked rice.

Makes 6 servings

Prep Time: 10 minutes
Cook Time: 25 minutes

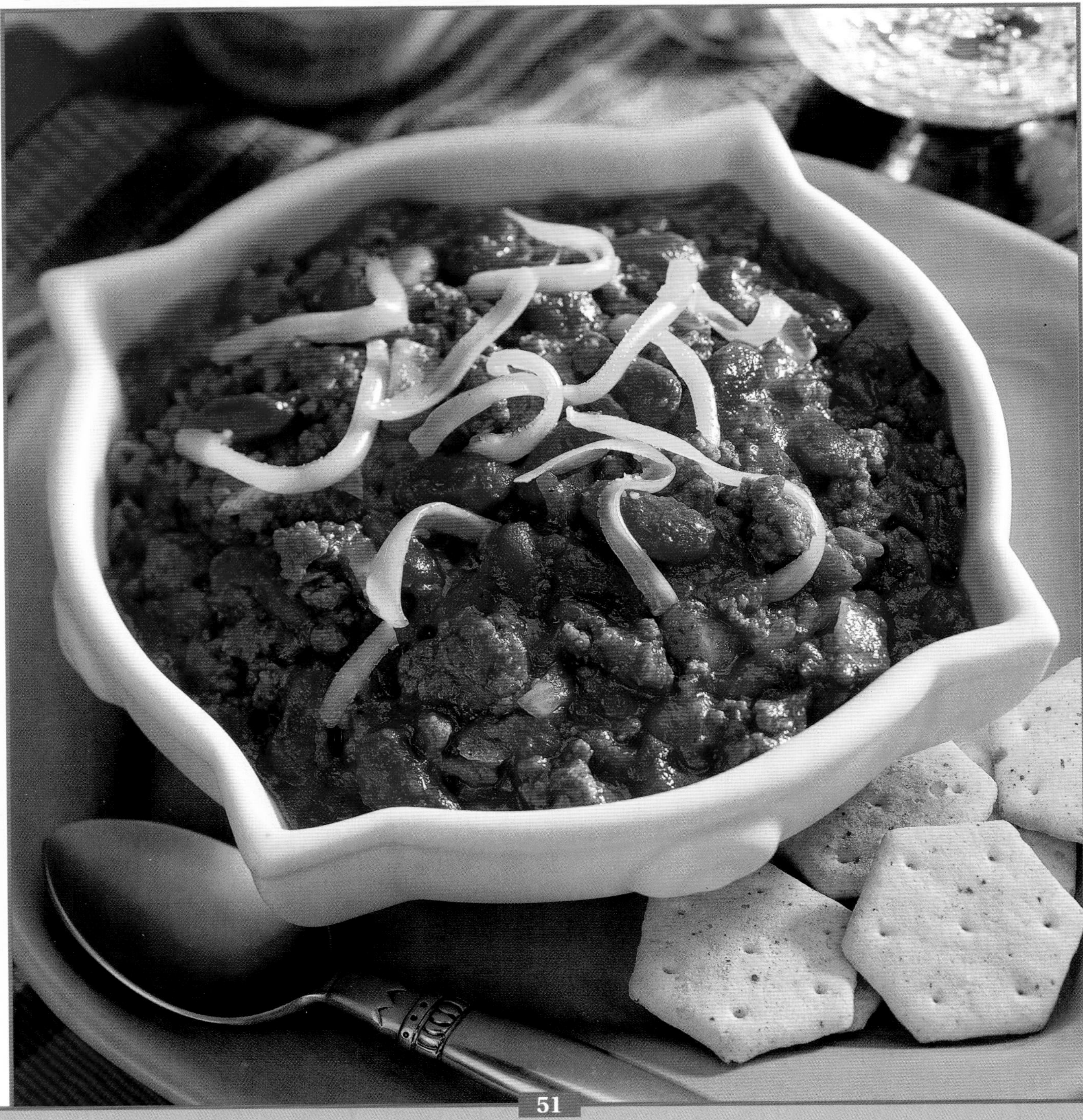

Quick Corn, Potato and Frank Soup

2 cans (about 15 ounces each) cream-style corn

2 cans (10½ ounces each) condensed chicken broth

2 cups frozen ready-to-cook hash browned potatoes with onions and peppers

½ teaspoon hot pepper sauce

1 package (12 ounces) HEBREW NATIONAL® Beef Franks, Reduced Fat Beef Franks or 97% Fat Free Beef Franks

½ cup sliced green onions, including tops

Combine corn, broth, potatoes with onions and peppers and hot sauce in large saucepan. Bring to a boil over high heat. Slice franks crosswise into ½-inch pieces; stir into broth mixture. Simmer, uncovered, 10 to 12 minutes. Stir in onions; simmer 3 minutes.

Makes 6 servings

Quick Tip

For carry-to-work lunches, prepare soup on the weekend. Divide into serving-size portions in individual plastic food storage containers. Store in the refrigerator or freezer until ready to use.

White Chicken Chili

1 to 2 tablespoons canola oil

1 onion, chopped (about 1 cup)

1 package (about 1¼ pounds) PERDUE® Fresh Ground Chicken, Turkey or Turkey Breast Meat

1 package (about 1¾ ounces) chili seasoning mix

1 can (14½ ounces) reduced-sodium chicken broth

1 can (15 ounces) cannellini or white kidney beans, drained and rinsed

In Dutch oven over medium-high heat, heat oil. Add onions; sauté 2 to 3 minutes, until softened and translucent. Add ground chicken; sauté 5 to 7 minutes, until no longer pink. Add chili mix and stir to combine. Add chicken broth and beans; bring to a boil. Reduce heat to medium-low; simmer 5 to 10 minutes, until all flavors are blended.

Makes 4 servings

Prep Time: 10 minutes
Cook Time: 10 to 20 minutes

Quick Corn, Potato and Frank Soup

Vegetable Chili

**2 cans (15 ounces each) chunky chili
tomato sauce**

**1 bag (16 ounces) BIRDS EYE® frozen Farm
Fresh Mixtures Broccoli, Corn and Red
Peppers**

1 can (15½ ounces) red kidney beans

1 can (4½ ounces) chopped green chilies

½ cup shredded Cheddar cheese

• Combine tomato sauce, vegetables, beans
and chilies in large saucepan; bring to a boil.

• Cook, uncovered, over medium heat
5 minutes.

• Sprinkle individual servings with cheese.

Makes 4 to 6 servings

Prep Time: 5 minutes
Cook Time: 10 minutes

Quick Tip

*Add a burst of flavor to soups by topping with
herbed croutons, tiny crackers, popcorn, corn chips,
bacon bits, Parmesan cheese or chopped fresh herbs.*

Jiffy Chicken & Rice Gumbo

**1 (6.9-ounce) package RICE-A-RONI®
Chicken Flavor**

**1 small green bell pepper, coarsely
chopped**

2 tablespoons margarine or butter

**1 pound boneless, skinless chicken
breasts, cut into 1-inch pieces**

**1 (14½-ounce) can diced tomatoes with
garlic and onion, undrained**

**¾ to 1 teaspoon Creole or Cajun
seasoning***

**½ teaspoon cayenne pepper, ¼ teaspoon dried oregano
and ¼ teaspoon dried thyme can be substituted.*

1. In large skillet over medium heat, sauté
rice-vermicelli mix and bell pepper with
margarine until vermicelli is golden brown.

2. Slowly stir in 2¼ cups water, chicken,
tomatoes, Creole seasoning and Special
Seasonings; bring to a boil. Reduce heat to
low. Cover; simmer 15 to 20 minutes or until
rice is tender. *Makes 4 servings*

Prep Time: 5 minutes
Cook Time: 30 minutes

Vegetable Chili

Southwestern Soup

1 bag (16 ounces) BIRDS EYE® frozen Corn

2 cans (15 ounces each) chili

1 cup hot water

½ cup chopped green bell pepper

- Combine all ingredients in saucepan.

- Cook over medium heat 10 to 12 minutes.

Makes 4 to 6 servings

Prep Time: 1 to 2 minutes
Cook Time: 10 to 12 minutes

Salsa Corn Soup with Chicken

3 quarts chicken broth

2 pounds boneless skinless chicken breasts, cooked and diced

2 packages (10 ounces each) frozen whole kernel corn, thawed

4 jars (11 ounces each) NEWMAN'S OWN® All Natural Salsa

4 large carrots, diced

Bring chicken broth to a boil in Dutch oven. Add chicken, corn, Newman's Own® Salsa and carrots. Bring to a boil. Reduce heat and simmer until carrots are tender.

Makes 8 servings

Hearty Turkey Cannellini Chili

1 pound ground turkey or ground beef

1 (6.9-ounce) package RICE-A-RONI® Chicken Flavor

2 tablespoons margarine or butter

1 (14½-ounce) can diced tomatoes with garlic and onion, undrained

1 tablespoon chili powder

1 (15-ounce) can cannellini beans, drained and rinsed

1. In large skillet over medium-high heat, cook ground turkey until no longer pink. Remove from skillet; drain. Set aside.

2. In same skillet over medium heat, sauté rice-vermicelli mix with margarine until vermicelli is golden brown.

3. Slowly stir in 2¼ cups water, tomatoes, chili powder and Special Seasonings; bring to a boil. Reduce heat to low. Cover; simmer 10 minutes.

4. Stir in beans and turkey; return to a simmer. Cover; simmer 5 to 7 minutes or until rice is tender. *Makes 6 servings*

Prep Time: 5 minutes
Cook Time: 30 minutes

Best Ever Beef Heroes

3 tablespoons mayonnaise

1 tablespoon Dijon mustard

2 teaspoons prepared horseradish

4 submarine or hoagie rolls, split

4 red leaf or romaine lettuce leaves

1 pound sliced deli roast beef

1 thin slice red onion, separated into rings

8 slices SARGENTO® Deli Style Sliced Swiss Cheese

1. Combine mayonnaise, mustard and horseradish; mix well. Spread on cut sides of rolls.

2. Fill rolls with lettuce, roast beef, onion rings and cheese. Close sandwiches; cut in half.

Makes 4 servings

Prep Time: *10 minutes*

Quick Tip

For grab-and-go lunches, prepare these sandwiches the night before. Individually wrap each sandwich so that they will be ready to pop into lunch bags the next morning.

Vegetarian Tacos

1 can (16 ounces) refried beans

1 onion, chopped

1 package (1.0 ounces) LAWRY'S® Taco Spices & Seasonings

1 large zucchini, coarsely grated

1 package (18 count) LAWRY'S® Taco Shells

1 can (2¼ ounces) sliced black olives, drained

2 medium tomatoes, chopped

Shredded lettuce

2 cups (8 ounces) shredded cheddar or Monterey Jack cheese

In medium saucepan, combine refried beans, onion, Taco Spices & Seasonings and ½ of zucchini; mix well. Bring to a boil over medium-high heat; reduce heat to low and simmer, uncovered, 3 minutes. Fill each Taco Shell with 2 to 3 tablespoons mixture. Place filled shells on baking sheet. Bake in 350°F oven 5 minutes. Top with olives, tomatoes, lettuce, remaining zucchini and cheese.

Makes 18 tacos

Serving Suggestion: Serve with a mixture of salsa and chopped avocado.

Croque Monsieur

8 slices firm white sandwich bread

2 tablespoons butter, softened

8 slices SARGENTO® Deli Style Sliced Swiss Cheese

2 tablespoons honey mustard

4 slices CURE 81® ham

4 slices cooked turkey breast

1. Spread one side of each slice of bread with butter; place butter side down on waxed paper. Top 4 slices of bread with 4 slices of cheese. Spread mustard over cheese; top with ham, turkey and remaining cheese. Close sandwiches with remaining bread, butter side out.

2. Heat a large skillet or griddle over medium heat until hot. Cook sandwiches in batches in skillet or on the griddle until golden brown, about 3 minutes per side.   *Makes 4 servings*

Prep Time: 8 minutes
Cook Time: 6 minutes

Quick Tip

Use small amounts of extra vegetables such as chopped tomato, red or green bell peppers or onions on sandwiches and quesadillas for added flavor and nutrition.

Caribbean Quesadillas

1 cup cut-up cooked chicken

1 tablespoon *Frank's® RedHot®* Cayenne Pepper Sauce

1 tablespoon lime juice

8 (6 inch) flour tortillas

4 tablespoons *French's®* Sweet & Tangy Honey Mustard

1 cup shredded cheese

1. Toss together chicken, ***Frank's RedHot*** Sauce and lime juice in medium bowl.

2. Spread each tortilla with *1 tablespoon* mustard. Sprinkle tortilla with cheese and top with chicken mixture, dividing evenly. Cover each with another tortilla, pressing down firmly to form quesadilla.

3. Coat large nonstick skillet with vegetable cooking spray. Cook quesadillas over medium heat about 2 to 3 minutes or until golden, turning once. Cut into wedges to serve.
Makes 4 servings

Prep Time: 10 minutes
Cook Time: about 10 minutes

Quick Tip

Keep fresh fruit, individual cans of fruit and small bags of chips or pretzels for easy-to-fill lunch bags.

Croque Monsieur

Baked Potatoes with Tuna and Broccoli in Cheese Sauce

2 medium baking potatoes (6 to 8 ounces each)

1 package (10 ounces) frozen broccoli in cheese sauce

1 (3-ounce) pouch of STARKIST® Premium Albacore Tuna

1 teaspoon chili powder

¼ cup minced green onions, including tops

2 slices cooked, crumbled bacon

Microwave Directions

Wash and pierce potatoes; microwave on HIGH 8 minutes. Wrap in foil; let stand to finish cooking while preparing broccoli. Microwave vented pouch of broccoli on HIGH 5 minutes. In medium microwavable bowl, combine tuna and chili powder. Gently stir in broccoli. Cover; heat on HIGH 1½ more minutes or until heated through. Cut potatoes in half lengthwise. Top with broccoli-tuna mixture; sprinkle with onions and bacon.

Makes 2 servings

Prep Time: 20 minutes

Quick Tip

This recipe can easily be doubled for four. Just cook a little longer in the microwave.

Philly Cheese Steak Sandwich

1 onion, sliced

1 green bell pepper, cut into thin strips

2 tablespoons butter or margarine

2 packages (6 ounces each) HILLSHIRE FARM® Deli Select Roast Beef, cut into thin strips

4 submarine or hoagie rolls, cut into halves

½ pound provolone cheese, sliced

Sauté onion and bell pepper in butter in medium saucepan over medium-high heat until onion is transparent. Mix in Roast Beef; heat until beef is warm. Evenly divide beef mixture into 4 portions; fill each roll with beef mixture. Top each sandwich evenly with cheese.

Makes 4 servings

Quick Tip

This easy-to-prepare warm sandwich also makes a quick evening meal. Serve with a leafy green salad and your favorite cookie.

Baked Potatoes with Tuna and Broccoli in Cheese Sauce

Riverside Fish Wraps

18 frozen breaded fish sticks

1 jar (10 ounces) LA CHOY® Sweet & Sour Sauce

⅓ cup Dijon mustard

6 burrito-size flour tortillas, warmed

1½ cups shredded lettuce

1 medium cucumber, peeled, seeded and julienned

Prepare fish sticks according to package directions; keep warm. Combine sweet and sour sauce and mustard; mix well. For each serving, spread about ¼ cup sweet and sour mixture evenly on each tortilla; top each with ¼ cup lettuce, evenly divided cucumber pieces and 3 fish sticks. Fold 2 opposite sides of each tortilla over ⅓ of filling. Roll each tortilla until filling is completely encased. To serve, cut each wrap diagonally.   *Makes 6 servings*

Muffaletta

8 ounces BUTTERBALL® Honey Roasted and Smoked Turkey Breast, sliced thin in the deli

8 ounces BUTTERBALL® Oven Roasted Turkey Breast, sliced thin in the deli

1½ cups prepared fat free Italian salad dressing

⅓ cup salad olives

1 large loaf crusty round Italian bread

½ pound sliced Swiss cheese

½ pound sliced provolone cheese

Leaf lettuce

2 large tomatoes, sliced

1 red onion, sliced thin

Combine salad dressing and olives in small bowl. Slice bread in half crosswise. Spoon ½ cup dressing on bottom half of bread. Layer turkey, cheeses, lettuce, tomatoes and onion onto bread. Pour remaining dressing on top half of bread; place on top. Cut into 16 pieces to serve.   *Makes 16 servings*

Prep Time: 15 minutes

Quick Tip

A muffaletta is a hero-style sandwich that originated in New Orleans. The crusty round loaf of bread and the olive salad make this sandwich different from other hero sandwiches.

California Garden Club

12 slices sourdough bread, toasted

1 (6-ounce) package FLEUR DE LAIT® Premium Light Spreading Cheese Crunchy Garden Vegetable cream cheese

¾ cup alfalfa sprouts

2 medium ripe tomatoes, sliced

6 grilled boneless chicken breast halves

1 avocado, peeled and sliced (optional)

Lay out 6 slices toasted sourdough bread on work surface.

Spread 2 tablespoons Fleur de Lait Crunchy Garden Vegetable cheese on each slice of bread and top each with 2 tablespoons sprouts. Place 2 slices tomato on top of sprouts and 1 lay chicken breast half over tomato slices.

Garnish each sandwich with 2 slices avocado and place other toasted bread slice over top. Halve and serve with vegetable slaw, pickled peppers or other crudités.

Makes 6 sandwiches

Grilled Wisconsin Triple Cheese Sandwich

12 slices whole grain bread

¼ cup whole grain Dijon style mustard

6 slices (1-ounce each) baked ham

6 slices (¾-ounce each) Wisconsin Provolone cheese

6 slices (¾-ounce each) Wisconsin Cheddar cheese

1 cup (6 ounces) crumbled Wisconsin Gorgonzola cheese

Prepare grill; heat until coals are ash white. Meanwhile, spread each slice of bread with mustard. Top each of 6 slices of bread with 1 slice ham, 1 slice Provolone and 1 slice Cheddar. Sprinkle with Gorgonzola cheese. Top each sandwich with remaining bread. Grill over hot coals, turning once, until cheese is melted, about 3 minutes per side.

Makes 6 sandwiches

Favorite recipe from **Wisconsin Milk Marketing Board**

Quick Tip

In the summer, fix these grilled sandwiches to get out of the hot kitchen. Serve sandwiches with pickle slices, raw vegetables, watermelon wedges and a brownie for an easy outdoor menu.

Rainbow Spirals

4 (10-inch) flour tortillas (assorted flavors and colors)

4 tablespoons *French's*® Mustard (any flavor)

½ pound (about 8 slices) thinly sliced deli roast beef, bologna or turkey

8 slices American, provolone or Muenster cheese

Fancy Party Toothpicks

1. Spread each tortilla with *1 tablespoon* mustard. Layer with meat and cheeses dividing evenly.

2. Roll up jelly-roll style; secure with toothpicks and cut into thirds. Arrange on platter.

Makes 4 to 6 servings

Quick and Hearty Deli Ham Sub

1 large sandwich roll, sliced in half lengthwise

Yellow or Dijon mustard, to taste

4 ounces HILLSHIRE FARM® Deli Select Brown Sugar Ham

2 ounces sliced American cheese

⅔ cup cole slaw

Dill pickle slices, to taste

Spread both cut sides of the roll with mustard to taste. Fill roll with the remaining ingredients. Slice in half and serve with your favorite chips.

Makes 1 sandwich

Smoked Turkey Roll-Ups

2 packages (4 ounces each) herb-flavored soft spreadable cheese

4 flour (8-inch diameter) tortillas*

2 packages (6 ounces each) smoked turkey breast slices

2 green onions, minced

¼ cup roasted red peppers, drained and finely chopped

To keep flour tortillas soft while preparing turkey roll-ups, cover with a slightly damp cloth.

1. Spread one package of cheese evenly over tortillas. Layer turkey slices evenly and over cheese, overlapping turkey slices slightly to cover each tortilla. Spread remaining package of cheese evenly over turkey slices. Sprinkle with green onions and red peppers.

2. Roll up each tortilla jelly-roll style. Place roll-ups, seam side down, in resealable plastic bag; refrigerate several hours or overnight.

3. To serve, cut each roll-up crosswise into ½-inch slices to form pinwheels. If desired, arrange pinwheels on serving plate and garnish with red pepper slices in center.

Makes 4 servings

Favorite recipe from **National Turkey Federation**

Feta Pockets

2 cups bean sprouts

1 small cucumber, chopped

½ cup (2 ounces) crumbled Wisconsin feta cheese

¼ cup plain low-fat yogurt

1 tablespoon sesame seeds, toasted

¼ teaspoon pepper

2 pita bread rounds, cut in half

1 medium tomato, cut into 4 slices

In medium bowl, stir together sprouts, cucumber, cheese, yogurt, sesame seeds and pepper. Spoon mixture into pita bread halves. Place tomato slice on filling in each bread half.

Makes 4 servings

Favorite recipe from **Wisconsin Milk Marketing Board**

Quick Tip

Feta cheese is a classic Greek cheese that is white and crumbly. Feta is a zesty addition to salads and sandwiches.

Texas Twister

1 package (10 ounces) PERDUE® SHORT CUTS® Fresh Mesquite Carved Chicken Breast

1 to 1½ cups prepared salsa (mild, medium or hot)

4 large (10- to 12-inch size) flour tortillas

1 cup shredded lettuce

⅓ cup sour cream

½ cup shredded Monterey Jack cheese

In medium saucepan over medium heat, combine chicken and salsa. Simmer 1 to 2 minutes until hot. Meanwhile, in large, nonstick skillet over medium-high heat, heat tortillas. Spread salsa and chicken on tortillas. Add lettuce, sour cream and cheese. Fold ends in and roll up to enclose filling.

Makes 4 servings

Variation: For an Italian twister, spread warm tortillas with mayonnaise and roll up carved Italian chicken breast or cut up CAFÉ PERDUE® Sun-Dried Tomato Turkey Breast. Add diced tomato, chopped olives and packaged, grated Italian cheese with herbs.

Prep Time: 6 to 8 minutes
Cook Time: 3 minutes

Feta Pocket

New Wave BLT

¼ **cup mayonnaise**

2 **tablespoons chopped fresh basil leaves**

8 **slices whole wheat bread, lightly toasted**

8 **slices crisply cooked bacon**

4 **slices large ripe tomato**

4 **slices SARGENTO® Deli Style Sliced Swiss Cheese**

4 **leaves romaine or red leaf lettuce**

Combine mayonnaise and basil; spread evenly over one side of each slice of toast. Layer bacon, tomato, cheese and lettuce on four slices of toast; close with remaining four slices of toast. Cut each sandwich diagonally in half.

Makes 4 servings

Prep Time: 20 minutes

Quick Tip

To cook bacon in a skillet, place in a single layer over medium-high heat, turning it 2 to 3 times for even cooking. To bake it, place bacon in a single layer on a rack in a baking pan and bake at 350°F 15 to 20 minutes or until crisp. Bacon also does well in the microwave. Just layer it between paper towels on a microwave-safe rack and microwave at HIGH (100%) about 1 minute per slice.

Saucy Pizza Pockets

⅓ **pound ground pork**

¼ **teaspoon garlic salt**

¾ **cup pizza sauce**

2 **(7½-ounce) packages refrigerated tube biscuits**

⅔ **cup shredded mozzarella cheese**

Slices of pepperoni or Canadian-style bacon

Heat oven to 425°F. Place ground pork and garlic salt in large skillet over medium-high heat; cook for 5 minutes, stirring occasionally, until pork is no longer pink. Stir in pizza sauce and cook, stirring, until heated through.

Spray two large baking sheets with nonstick cooking spray. Arrange biscuits on baking sheets, leaving space between each. Flatten biscuits with hands. Spoon 1 tablespoon meat sauce onto center of half of the biscuits. Sprinkle with 1 tablespoon cheese, top with slice of pepperoni or Canadian-style bacon. Carefully top with remaining biscuits; seal outside edges of biscuits by pressing down with the tines of a fork. Bake for 10 to 13 minutes, or until golden brown.

Makes 8 snack servings

Favorite recipe from **National Pork Board**

Ragú® Pizza Burgers

1 pound ground beef

2 cups RAGÚ® Old World Style® Pasta Sauce, divided

1 cup shredded mozzarella cheese (about 4 ounces), divided

¼ teaspoon salt

6 English muffins, split and toasted

1. In small bowl, combine ground beef, ½ cup Ragú Pasta Sauce, ½ cup cheese and salt. Shape into 6 patties. Grill or broil until done.

2. Meanwhile, heat remaining 1½ cups pasta sauce. To serve, arrange burgers on muffin halves. Top with remaining ½ cup cheese, sauce and muffin halves.   *Makes 6 servings*

Prep Time: 10 minutes
Cook Time: 15 minutes

Quick Tip

Ground beef patties should be cooked to 160°F. The interior of these burgers may remain pink because of the pasta sauce. To insure doneness, check the internal temperature with a quick read thermometer or cook ½-inch-thick patties 10 to 12 minutes over medium heat.

Smoked Ham & Roasted Red Pepper Roll-Ups

⅔ cup cream cheese, softened

½ cup shredded mozzarella or Cheddar cheese

½ cup chopped roasted red peppers, drained

¼ cup *French's*® Bold n' Spicy Brown Mustard

6 (10-inch) flour tortillas

¾ pound thinly sliced smoked ham

1. Beat cream cheese, mozzarella cheese, red peppers and mustard in medium bowl until smooth. Spread about ¼ *cup* mixture evenly on each tortilla.

2. Arrange ham on top. Roll up tortillas jelly-roll style. Cut into 2-inch pieces.
Makes 6 servings

Prep Time: 15 minutes

Quick Tip

Keep a jar of roasted red peppers on hand to use as a delicious ingredient in salads and sandwiches.

Ragú® Pizza Burgers

Provolone Tuna Melts

1 can (12 ounces) white tuna in water, drained

¼ cup diced drained bottled roasted red bell peppers

¼ cup chopped pitted kalamata or ripe olives

3 tablespoons creamy Caesar salad dressing or mayonnaise

1 tablespoon chopped fresh basil or parsley

4 large slices Vienna or sourdough bread, lightly toasted

8 slices SARGENTO® Deli Style Sliced Provolone Cheese

1. Combine tuna, bell peppers, olives, dressing and basil; mix well. Spread mixture evenly over toast; top with cheese, overlapping as necessary to cover filling and edges of toast.

2. Place on a foil-lined baking sheet; broil 4 to 5 inches from heat source until cheese melts and sandwich is hot, 2 to 3 minutes.

Makes 4 servings

Prep Time: 10 minutes
Cook Time: 3 minutes

Buffalo-Style Wraps

⅔ cup *Frank's® RedHot®* Cayenne Pepper Sauce

1 pound boneless skinless chicken breast halves

¼ cup blue cheese salad dressing

4 (10-inch) flour tortillas, heated

1 cup shredded cheese

1 cup shredded lettuce

1. Pour ⅓ *cup Frank's RedHot* Sauce over chicken in deep dish; cover. Marinate in refrigerator 30 minutes.

2. Grill or broil chicken 10 minutes or until no longer pink in center. Cut chicken into strips. Toss chicken with blue cheese dressing and remaining ⅓ *cup Frank's RedHot* Sauce.

3. Top tortillas with chicken, cheese and lettuce. Roll up to enclose filling. Cut in half to serve.

Makes 4 servings

Prep Time: 10 minutes
Marinate Time: 30 minutes
Cook Time: 10 minutes

Provolone Tuna Melts

Skillet Sloppy Joes

1 pound lean ground beef

1 can (15 ounces) Sloppy Joe sandwich sauce

1⅓ cups *French's®* French Fried Onions, divided

½ cup (2 ounces) shredded Cheddar cheese

4 Kaiser or hamburger rolls, split

1. Cook ground beef in skillet over medium-high heat until browned and no longer pink; drain. Stir in sauce; cover and simmer over medium heat 5 minutes.

2. Stir in ⅔ *cup* French Fried Onions. Top with cheese; cover and let stand 1 minute or until cheese is melted.

3. Spoon beef mixture onto bottoms of rolls. Sprinkle with remaining onions and cover with roll tops. Serve immediately.

Makes 4 servings

Tip: For spicier flavor, add 1 to 2 tablespoons *Frank's® RedHot®* **Cayenne Pepper Sauce.**

Variation: For added Cheddar flavor, substitute *French's®* new **Cheddar French Fried Onions** for the original flavor.

Prep Time: 5 minutes
Cook Time: 12 minutes

Crispy Parmesan-Peppercorn Pita Sandwiches

1 package (14 ounces) BUTTERBALL® Chicken Requests™ Parmesan Crispy Baked Breasts

4 large pitas

½ cup sprouts

¼ red onion, thin sliced, separated into rings

¼ cup prepared peppercorn ranch salad dressing

Prepare chicken according to package directions. Cut one inch off top of each pita; open. Place chicken breasts, sprouts, onion and dressing in pitas.   *Makes 4 sandwiches*

Prep Time: 20 minutes

Quick Tip

Pita bread, either white or whole wheat, is sometimes called pocket bread. Ideal for sandwiches, pita rounds can be filled in the center and folded up like a taco or split horizontally to open the pocket which can be stuffed with a variety of fillings.

Skillet Sloppy Joe

Garlic Turkey Pocket Pita

1 large whole-wheat pita bread, cut in half

6 ounces HILLSHIRE FARM® Deli Select Garlic Turkey

1 cup finely shredded romaine lettuce

½ cup diced tomatoes, salted to taste

½ cup shredded carrots

3 tablespoons Ranch Dressing (regular or reduced fat)

Open the pockets of the two pita halves.

Arrange half of the Garlic Turkey in each pocket.

Toss the lettuce, tomatoes and carrots with the Ranch Dressing.

Spoon half of the mixture into each pocket, distributing evenly.

Serve immediately.   *Makes 1 to 2 servings*

Easy Onion Tacos

1½ pounds ground beef

1 envelope LIPTON® RECIPE SECRETS® Onion Soup Mix

1½ cups prepared salsa

1 package (4.8 ounces) taco shells, heated, if desired

1. In 12-inch skillet, brown ground beef over medium-high heat; drain.

2. Stir in soup mix and salsa. Bring to a boil over high heat.

3. Reduce heat to low and simmer uncovered, stirring occasionally, 10 minutes or until thickened. Serve in warm taco shells. Top, if desired, with your favorite taco toppings.

Makes 10 tacos

Prep Time: 5 minutes
Cook Time: 15 minutes

Chicken Pizzawiches

1 package (12 ounces) frozen breaded chicken breast patties

1 cup (4 ounces) shredded mozzarella cheese

1 jar (14 ounces) spaghetti sauce

½ cup HOLLAND HOUSE® Red Cooking Wine

4 sandwich buns

Microwave Directions

Microwave chicken patties as directed on package. Top with cheese. Microwave on HIGH an additional 30 to 60 seconds.

Microwave combined spaghetti sauce and cooking wine in microwavable bowl covered with waxed paper 4 to 5 minutes, stirring once. Place chicken patties in buns; spoon sauce over patties.   *Makes 4 servings*

Zesty Pasta Salad

3 cups uncooked rotini pasta

1 cup olive oil vinaigrette salad dressing

¼ cup *French's®* Bold n' Spicy Brown Mustard

¼ cup chopped fresh basil *or* 2 teaspoons dried basil leaves

1⅓ cups *French's®* French Fried Onions, divided

2 cups cut-up fresh vegetables, such as broccoli, carrots, zucchini, sugar snap peas

Cook pasta according to package directions using shortest cooking time. Drain; rinse under cold running water.

Combine salad dressing, mustard and basil in small bowl; mix well. Combine pasta, ⅔ *cup* French Fried Onions and vegetables in large bowl. Pour dressing mixture over salad; toss well to coat evenly. Cover; refrigerate until ready to serve. Sprinkle with remaining ⅔ *cup* onions just before serving.

Makes 8 servings

Prep Time: 10 minutes
Cook Time: 10 minutes

Beef Caesar Salad

2 pounds boneless beef sirloin, top round
    or flank steak
1 bottle (8 ounces) creamy Caesar salad
    dressing
¼ cup *French's*® Worcestershire Sauce
¼ cup *French's*® Napa Valley Style Dijon
    Mustard
1 teaspoon grated lemon peel
2 tablespoons lemon juice
8 cups romaine lettuce leaves, washed
    and torn

1. Place steak in resealable plastic food storage bag. Combine remaining ingredients *except* lettuce. Pour ¾ *cup* Worcestershire mixture over steak. Seal bag; marinate steak in refrigerator 30 minutes. Reserve remaining sauce for dressing.

2. Broil or grill steak 15 minutes for medium-rare. Let stand 15 minutes. Slice steak; serve with dressing over lettuce.

Makes 8 servings

Prep Time: 35 minutes
Cook Time: 15 minutes

Classic Italian Pasta Salad

8 ounces uncooked rotelle or spiral pasta
2½ cups assorted cut-up fresh vegetables
    (broccoli, carrots, tomatoes, bell
    peppers, cauliflower, onions and
    mushrooms)
½ cup cubed cheddar or mozzarella cheese
⅓ cup sliced pitted ripe olives (optional)
1 cup WISH-BONE® Creamy Caesar
    Dressing*

*Also terrific with WISH-BONE® Italian, Robusto Italian, Fat Free Italian, Classic House Italian, Creamy Roasted Garlic, Red Wine Vinaigrette or Fat Free Red Wine Vinaigrette Dressing.

Cook pasta according to package directions; drain and rinse with cold water until completely cool.

In large bowl, combine all ingredients except creamy Caesar dressing. Add dressing; toss well. Serve chilled or at room temperature.

Makes 8 side-dish servings

Note: If preparing a day ahead, refrigerate, then stir in ¼ cup additional Wish-Bone® Dressing before serving.

Beef Caesar Salad

Southwest Caesar Salad

1 package (10 ounces) DOLE® Complete
    Caesar Salad

2 cups cubed cooked chicken breast

1 can (14 to 16 ounces) low-sodium
    kidney, black or pinto beans, drained

1 can (8 ounces) low-sodium whole kernel
    corn, drained

1 medium tomato, cut into wedges

1 medium DOLE® Red, Yellow or Green
    Bell Pepper, thinly sliced

½ medium onion, thinly sliced

• Combine romaine, croutons and Parmesan
cheese from salad bag with chicken, beans,
corn, tomato, bell pepper and onion in large
serving bowl.

• Pour dressing from packet over salad; toss to
evenly coat.   *Makes 4 servings*

Note: Refrigerate salad blends, complete
salads and vegetable combinations in their
original bags as soon as you get them home.
Since the bags have been designed with a
special material to keep vegetables at their
freshest, you can store any leftovers in the
same bags, tightly closed, in your refrigerator
crisper.

Prep Time: 10 minutes

Pineapple Chicken Salad

1 packet (1 ounce) HIDDEN VALLEY®
    The Original Ranch® Salad Dressing
    & Seasoning Mix

½ cup mayonnaise

¼ cup pineapple juice

2 cups cubed, cooked chicken

1 cup sliced celery

1 can (20 ounces) pineapple chunks
    (reserve juice for above)

Combine dressing mix with mayonnaise and
pineapple juice. Add chicken, celery and
pineapple to mixture and toss well to coat.
Chill.   *Makes 4 to 6 servings*

Quick Tip

*Consider a main dish salad for your next potluck.
Quick, convenient and fresh, a salad will be the star
of the event.*

Southwest Caesar Salad

Three-Pepper Pizza

1 cup (½ of 15 ounce can) CONTADINA® Four Cheese Pizza Sauce

1 (12-inch) prepared pre-baked pizza crust

1½ cups (6 ounces) shredded mozzarella cheese, divided

½ each: red, green and yellow bell peppers, sliced into thin rings

2 tablespoons shredded Parmesan cheese

1 tablespoon chopped fresh basil *or* 1 teaspoon dried basil leaves, crushed

1. Spread pizza sauce onto crust to within 1 inch of edge.

2. Sprinkle with 1 cup mozzarella cheese, bell peppers, remaining mozzarella cheese and Parmesan cheese.

3. Bake according to pizza crust package directions or until crust is crisp and cheese is melted. Sprinkle with basil.

Makes 8 servings

BelGioioso® Provolone Pita Pizzas

1 pita bread

⅔ cup pizza sauce

¼ cup diced onion

¼ cup diced green bell pepper

10 to 12 thin slices pepperoni

1 cup shredded BELGIOIOSO® Provolone Cheese

Split pita into 2 rounds. (If pita doesn't separate, use 2 whole pitas.) Place pitas cut-side up on baking pan. Layer each pita with pizza sauce, onion, bell pepper, pepperoni and BelGioioso Provolone Cheese. Bake in preheated 400°F oven 7 to 8 minutes. Cut each pita into 4 pieces. *Makes 2 servings*

Quick Tip

Pizzas can be made using a variety of breads for the crust. Try tortillas for a thin crispy crust, pita breads for a more substantial crust or English muffins and bagels for mini snack pizzas.

Three-Pepper Pizza

Buffalo Chicken Pizza

1 can (10 ounces) refrigerated pizza dough
¾ cup RAGÚ® Pizza Quick® Sauce
2 cups diced cooked chicken
½ cup chopped celery
1 to 3 teaspoons hot pepper sauce
½ cup crumbled blue cheese

1. Preheat oven to 450°F. On greased 10-inch pizza pan, press dough to edge of pan.

2. In medium bowl, combine Ragú Pizza Quick Sauce, chicken, celery and hot pepper sauce. Spread mixture over pizza dough, then sprinkle with cheese. Bake 10 minutes or until crust is golden. *Makes 4 servings*

Prep Time: 10 minutes
Cook Time: 10 minutes

Quick Tip

For a crispy crust and great flavor, try putting the pizza directly on the grill or the oven rack.

Manwich Pizza

1 can (15.5 ounces) HUNT'S® Manwich Original Sloppy Joe Sauce
2 (12-inch each) prepared pizza shells
12 ounces bulk sausage, cooked and crumbled
2 cups shredded mozzarella cheese, divided

Spread ½ can Manwich Sauce over each pizza shell. Top each pizza evenly with 1 cup sausage and 1 cup cheese. Bake at 400°F 10 minutes. Cut each pizza into 8 wedges.
Makes 2 pizzas

Quick Tip

A pizza wheel is a handy utensil for quickly cutting pizza into pieces. Choose a wheel with a heavy-duty sharp blade.

Buffalo Chicken Pizza

Rush Hour Dinners

Ragú® Chili Mac

1 tablespoon BERTOLLI® Olive Oil
1 medium green bell pepper, chopped
1 pound ground beef
1 jar (1 pound 10 ounces) RAGÚ® Old World Style® Pasta Sauce
2 tablespoons chili powder
8 ounces elbow macaroni, cooked and drained

1. In 12-inch nonstick skillet, heat oil over medium-high heat and cook green bell pepper, stirring occasionally, 3 minutes. Add ground beef and brown, stirring occasionally; drain.

2. Stir in Ragú Pasta Sauce and chili powder. Bring to a boil over high heat. Reduce heat to low and simmer covered 10 minutes.

3. Stir in macaroni and heat through. Serve, if desired, with sour cream and shredded Cheddar cheese.

Makes 4 servings

Prep Time: 10 minutes
Cook Time: 25 minutes

Ragú® Chili Mac

Teriyaki Beef

¾ **pound top sirloin steak, cut into thin strips**

½ **cup teriyaki sauce**

¼ **cup water**

1 **tablespoon cornstarch**

1 **teaspoon sugar**

1 **bag (16 ounces) BIRDS EYE® frozen Farm Fresh Mixtures Broccoli, Carrots and Water Chestnuts**

• Spray large skillet with nonstick cooking spray; cook beef strips over medium-high heat 7 to 8 minutes, stirring occasionally.

• Combine teriyaki sauce, water, cornstarch and sugar; mix well.

• Add teriyaki sauce mixture and vegetables to beef. Bring to boil; quickly reduce heat to medium.

• Cook 7 to 10 minutes or until broccoli is heated through, stirring occasionally.

Makes 4 to 6 servings

Serving Suggestion: Serve this Oriental favorite on a bed of rice and garnish with chow mein noodles or toasted sesame seeds.

Prep Time: 5 to 10 minutes
Cook Time: 20 minutes

Mexican Lasagna

1 **jar (1 pound 10 ounces) RAGÚ® Old World Style® Pasta Sauce**

1 **pound ground beef**

1 **can (15¼ ounces) whole kernel corn, drained**

4½ **teaspoons chili powder**

6 **(8½-inch) flour tortillas**

2 **cups shredded Cheddar cheese (about 8 ounces)**

1. Preheat oven to 350°F. Set aside 1 cup Ragú Pasta Sauce. In 10-inch skillet, brown ground beef over medium-high heat; drain. Stir in remaining Ragú Pasta Sauce, corn and chili powder.

2. In 13×9-inch baking dish, spread 1 cup sauce mixture. Arrange two tortillas over sauce, overlapping edges slightly. Layer half the sauce mixture and ⅓ of the cheese over tortillas; repeat layers, ending with tortillas. Spread tortillas with reserved sauce.

3. Bake 30 minutes, then top with remaining cheese and bake an additional 10 minutes or until sauce is bubbling and cheese is melted.

Makes 8 servings

Variation: Substitute refried beans for ground beef for a meatless main dish.

Prep Time: 20 minutes
Cook Time: 40 minutes

Teriyaki Beef

Steakhouse London Broil

1 package KNORR® Recipe Classics™
    Roasted Garlic Herb or French Onion
    Soup, Dip and Recipe Mix
⅓ cup BERTOLLI® Olive Oil
2 tablespoons red wine vinegar
1 (1½- to 2-pound) beef round steak (for
    London Broil) or flank steak

• In large plastic food storage bag or
13×9-inch glass baking dish, blend recipe
mix, oil and vinegar.

• Add steak, turning to coat. Close bag, or
cover, and marinate in refrigerator 30 minutes
to 3 hours.

• Remove meat from marinade, discarding
marinade. Grill or broil, turning occasionally,
until desired doneness.

• Slice meat thinly across the grain.
Makes 6 to 8 servings

Garlic Chicken: Substitute 6 to 8 boneless
chicken breasts or 3 to 4 pounds bone-in
chicken pieces for steak. Marinate as directed.
Grill boneless chicken breasts 6 minutes or
bone-in chicken pieces 20 minutes or until
chicken is thoroughly cooked.

Prep Time: 5 minutes
Marinate Time: 30 minutes to 3 hours
Grill Time: 20 minutes

Tacos Olé

1 pound ground beef or turkey
1 cup salsa
¼ cup *Frank's® RedHot®* Cayenne Pepper
    Sauce
2 teaspoons ground chili powder
8 taco shells, heated
1⅓ cups *French's®* French Fried Onions

1. Cook beef in skillet over medium-high heat
until browned; drain. Stir in salsa, *Frank's
RedHot* Sauce and chili powder. Heat to
boiling. Reduce heat; cook 5 minutes, stirring
often.

2. To serve, spoon meat mixture into taco
shells. Top with French Fried Onions. Splash
on more *Frank's RedHot* Sauce to taste.
Garnish as desired. *Makes 4 servings*

Prep Time: 5 minutes
Cook Time: 10 minutes

Quick Tip

*An easy way to add more vegetables to your diet is to
add small amounts of grated vegetables to taco
fillings. Cook and stir a grated carrot with the
ground beef. The filling will taste great and your
family won't even know they are eating vegetables.*

Steakhouse London Broil

Beef & Broccoli Pepper Steak

3 tablespoons margarine or butter, divided

1 pound sirloin or top round steak, cut into thin strips

1 (6.8-ounce) package RICE-A-RONI® Beef Flavor

2 cups broccoli flowerets

½ cup red or green bell pepper strips

1 small onion, thinly sliced

1. In large skillet over medium-high heat, melt 1 tablespoon margarine. Add steak; sauté 3 minutes or until just browned. Remove from skillet; set aside.

2. In same skillet over medium heat, sauté rice-vermicelli mix with remaining 2 tablespoons margarine until vermicelli is golden brown. Slowly stir in 2½ cups water and Special Seasonings; bring to a boil. Reduce heat to low. Cover; simmer 10 minutes.

3. Stir in steak, broccoli, bell pepper and onion; return to a simmer. Cover; simmer 5 to 10 minutes or until rice is tender.

Makes 4 servings

Prep Time: 10 minutes
Cook Time: 30 minutes

Taco Burgers

2 pounds ground beef

1 envelope LIPTON® RECIPE SECRETS® Onion Soup Mix*

½ cup finely chopped green bell pepper

1 medium tomato, chopped

2 teaspoons chili powder

Also terrific with Lipton® Recipe Secrets® Beefy Onion or Beefy Mushroom Soup Mix.

In large bowl, combine all ingredients; shape into 12 oblong burgers. Grill or broil until meat is no longer pink. Serve, if desired, in taco shells or frankfurter rolls and top with shredded lettuce and shredded Cheddar cheese. *Makes 8 to 12 servings*

Quick Tip

To save leftover hamburgers, wrap each burger tightly in foil and freeze up to 4 months. Defrost in the refrigerator and reheat to 165°F for a just-grilled taste.

Beef & Broccoli Pepper Steak

Sizzle Marinated Steak

2 pounds boneless sirloin or top round steak
½ cup *French's*® Worcestershire Sauce
½ cup red wine vinegar
¼ cup *French's*® Napa Valley Style Dijon Mustard
¼ cup olive oil
1 teaspoon minced garlic

1. Place steak into deep dish or resealable plastic food storage bag.

2. Combine remaining ingredients in small bowl. Pour over steak. Marinate in refrigerator 30 minutes. Broil or grill about 5 minutes per side or until desired doneness. Serve with Signature Steak Sauce.   *Makes 8 servings*

Signature Steak Sauce: Combine ½ cup ketchup, ¼ cup *French's*® Worcestershire Sauce, 1 tablespoon *Frank's*® *RedHot*® Sauce and 1 teaspoon minced garlic in small bowl until well blended.

Marinate Time: 30 minutes
Prep Time: 5 minutes
Cook Time: 10 minutes

Zesty Onion Meatloaf

2 pounds ground beef
1⅓ cups *French's*® French Fried Onions
1 cup spaghetti sauce, divided
½ cup bread crumbs
¼ cup *French's*® Worcestershire Sauce
2 eggs

1. Preheat oven to 350°F. Thoroughly mix beef, ⅔ *cup* French Fried Onions, ½ *cup* sauce, bread crumbs, Worcestershire Sauce and eggs in large bowl.

2. Shape into loaf in baking dish. Bake 1 hour or until thoroughly cooked and internal temperature reaches 160°F; drain. Top with remaining ½ *cup* sauce and ⅔ *cup* onions. Bake 5 minutes or until onions are golden.
Makes 6 to 8 servings

Prep Time: 10 minutes
Cook Time: about 1 hour

Quick Tip

An instant-read thermometer is a handy kitchen tool to check the internal temperature of foods. Since the interior of a meatloaf may remain pink or red because of the spaghetti sauce, you can check the doneness by inserting an instant-read thermometer into the center of the meatloaf at the end of cooking time. The temperature should be 160°F or above. Do not leave the thermometer in the meatloaf while in the oven.

Cheeseburger Macaroni Stew

1 pound ground beef

1 can (28 ounces) crushed tomatoes in puree

1½ cups uncooked elbow macaroni

2 tablespoons *French's*® Worcestershire Sauce

1 cup shredded Cheddar cheese

1½ cups *French's*® French Fried Onions

1. Cook meat in large nonstick skillet over medium-high heat until browned and no longer pink; drain.

2. Add tomatoes, macaroni and *1½ cups water.* Bring to boiling. Boil, partially covered, 10 minutes until macaroni is tender. Stir in Worcestershire.

3. Sprinkle with cheese and French Fried Onions. *Makes 6 servings*

Variation: For a Southwestern flavor, add 2 tablespoons chili powder to ground beef and substitute 2 tablespoons *Frank's*® RedHot Sauce for the Worcestershire.

Prep Time: 5 minutes
Cook Time: 15 minutes

Rosemary Garlic Rub

2 tablespoons chopped fresh rosemary

1½ teaspoons LAWRY'S® Seasoned Salt

1 teaspoon LAWRY'S® Garlic Pepper

½ teaspoon LAWRY'S® Garlic Powder with Parsley

1 pound beef top sirloin steak

1 tablespoon olive oil

In small bowl, combine rosemary, Seasoned Salt, Garlic Pepper and Garlic Powder with Parsley; mix well. Brush both sides of steak with oil. Sprinkle with herb mixture, pressing onto steak. Grill or broil steak 15 to 20 minutes or until desired doneness, turning halfway through grilling time. *Makes 4 servings*

Meal Idea: Serve with oven roasted or French fried potatoes and honey-coated carrots.

Prep Time: 2 minutes
Cook Time: 15 to 20 minutes

Quick Tip

This rub is also great on other tender meat cuts such as beef rib eye, beef top loin (strip) steak, beef T-Bone steak, pork tenderloin, pork loin chops or lamb chops.

Coriander-Pepper Chops

4 boneless pork chops, 1-inch thick

1 tablespoon crushed coriander seeds

1 tablespoon brown sugar

2 cloves garlic, crushed

1 tablespoon coarsely ground black pepper

3 tablespoons low-sodium soy sauce

Combine all ingredients except pork chops. Place chops in a shallow dish and pour marinade over; let marinate 30 minutes. Prepare medium-hot coals in grill bed. Remove pork from marinade, discarding marinade, and grill chops for 7 to 8 minutes, turning once. Or broil chops 3 to 4 inches from heat source 7 to 8 minutes, turning once.

Makes 4 servings

Favorite recipe from **National Pork Board**

Quick Tip

For easy cleanup, put the marinade and chops in a resealable plastic food storage bag. Just throw the bag away after removing the chops from the marinade.

Garlic Pork Chops

6 bone-in pork chops, ¾ inch thick

1 envelope LIPTON® RECIPE SECRETS® Savory Herb with Garlic Soup Mix

2 tablespoons vegetable oil

½ cup hot water

1. Preheat oven to 425°F. In broiler pan, without the rack, arrange chops. Brush both sides of chops with soup mix combined with oil.

2. Bake chops 25 minutes or until barely pink in center.

3. Remove chops to serving platter. Add hot water to pan and stir, scraping brown bits from bottom of pan. Serve sauce over chops.

Makes 4 servings

Prep Time: 5 minutes
Cook Time: 25 minutes

Garlic Pork Chop

Lit'l Smokies 'n' Macaroni 'n' Cheese

1 package (7¼ ounces) macaroni and
  cheese mix, prepared according to
  package directions
1 pound HILLSHIRE FARM® Lit'l Smokies
1 can (10¾ ounces) condensed cream of
  celery or mushroom soup, undiluted
⅓ cup milk
1 tablespoon minced parsley (optional)
1 cup (4 ounces) shredded Cheddar cheese

Preheat oven to 350°F.

Combine prepared macaroni and cheese, Lit'l
Smokies, soup, milk and parsley, if desired, in
medium bowl. Pour into small greased
casserole. Sprinkle Cheddar cheese over top.
Bake, uncovered, 20 minutes or until heated
through.   *Makes 8 servings*

Honey-Mustard Tenderloin

1 whole pork tenderloin, about 1 pound
4 tablespoons honey
2 tablespoons brown sugar
2 tablespoons cider vinegar
1 tablespoon Dijon mustard

Combine all ingredients except tenderloin;
coat tenderloin well with sauce. Roast in
400°F oven for 20 to 30 minutes, basting
occasionally, until meat thermometer registers
160°F. Slice thinly to serve.

Makes 4 servings

Favorite recipe from **National Pork Board**

Quick Tip

*Pork tenderloins weigh about ¾ to 1 pound. They are
often sold with two tenderloins per package.*

Lit'l Smokies 'n' Macaroni 'n' Cheese

Glazed Pork Chops & Apples

4 boneless pork chops, ½ inch thick

½ cup apple juice

¼ cup *French's®* Bold n' Spicy Brown Mustard

¼ cup packed brown sugar

1 green or red apple, cut into small chunks

1. Heat *1 tablespoon oil* in nonstick skillet over medium-high heat. Cook pork chops for 5 minutes or until browned on both sides.

2. Add remaining ingredients. Bring to a full boil. Reduce heat to medium. Simmer, uncovered, for 8 to 10 minutes or until pork is no longer pink in center and sauce thickens slightly, stirring occasionally.

3. Serve with noodles, if desired.

Makes 4 servings

Prep Time: 5 minutes
Cook Time: 13 minutes

Quick Tip

Fix a green vegetable or salad while the pork chops are cooking. You'll have dinner on the table in 25 minutes.

Family Baked Bean Dinner

1 can (20 ounces) DOLE® Pineapple Chunks

½ DOLE® Green Bell Pepper, julienne-cut

½ cup chopped onion

1 pound Polish sausage or frankfurters, cut into 1-inch chunks

⅓ cup packed brown sugar

1 teaspoon dry mustard

2 cans (16 ounces each) baked beans

Microwave Directions

• Drain pineapple chunks; reserve juice for beverage. Add green pepper and onion to 13×9-inch microwavable dish.

• Cover; microwave on HIGH (100% power) 3 minutes. Add sausage, arranging around edges of dish. Cover; continue microwaving on HIGH (100% power) 6 minutes.

• In bowl, combine brown sugar and mustard; stir in beans and pineapple. Add to sausage mixture. Stir to combine. Microwave, uncovered, on HIGH (100% power) 8 to 10 minutes, stirring after 4 minutes.

Makes 6 servings

Glazed Pork Chop & Apples

Orange Chicken Piccata

1 pound boneless skinless chicken breasts, pounded thin

2 tablespoons flour

½ cup orange juice

¼ cup *French's*® Sweet & Tangy Honey Mustard

¼ cup orange marmalade

¼ teaspoon rosemary leaves, crushed

1 orange, thinly sliced and quartered

1. Coat chicken with flour; shake off excess. Heat *1 tablespoon oil* in nonstick skillet. Cook chicken 5 minutes or until browned.

2. Mix orange juice, mustard, marmalade and rosemary. Add to skillet. Bring to boiling. Simmer, uncovered, over medium-low heat for 5 minutes or until chicken is no longer pink in center and sauce thickens slightly.

3. Stir in orange pieces; heat through. Serve with rice if desired.   *Makes 4 servings*

Prep Time: 5 minutes
Cook Time: 10 minutes

Southwestern Chicken

1 cup prepared Italian salad dressing

1 tablespoon lime juice

1 tablespoon *French's*® Sweet & Tangy Honey Mustard

1 pound thinly sliced chicken cutlets

1⅓ cups *French's*® French Fried Onions

1 cup (4 ounces) shredded Cheddar cheese

1. Combine salad dressing, lime juice and mustard in small bowl. Pour marinade over chicken in deep dish. Cover and marinate in refrigerator 30 minutes or up to 1 hour.

2. Heat 3 tablespoons marinade in 12-inch nonstick skillet over high heat. Cook chicken 5 minutes or until chicken is no longer pink in center, turning once. (Discard remaining marinade.)

3. Sprinkle French Fried Onions and cheese over chicken. Cook, covered, 2 minutes or until cheese is melted.   *Makes 4 servings*

Prep Time: 5 minutes
Marinate Time: 30 minutes
Cook Time: 7 minutes

Quick Tip

Pounding boned chicken breasts to a uniform thickness, usually ¼ inch, allows them to cook faster and more evenly. Place the chicken between two pieces of plastic wrap to prevent it from tearing. Using the flat bottom (not the edge) of a meat pounder or a rolling pin, pound the chicken with a downward motion until it is evenly flattened.

Orange Chicken Piccata

Country French Chicken Skillet

2 tablespoons margarine or butter

1½ pounds boneless, skinless chicken breast halves

1 cup water

1 package KNORR® Recipe Classics™ Vegetable or Spring Vegetable Soup, Dip and Recipe Mix

¼ teaspoon dried dill weed (optional)

½ cup sour cream

• In large skillet, melt margarine over medium-high heat and brown chicken, turning occasionally, 5 minutes.

• Stir in water, recipe mix and dill weed. Bring to a boil over high heat. Reduce heat to low and simmer covered, stirring occasionally, 10 minutes or until chicken is thoroughly cooked. Remove chicken to serving platter and keep warm.

• Remove skillet from heat; stir in sour cream. Spoon sauce over chicken and serve, if desired, with noodles.   *Makes 4 to 6 servings*

Prep Time: 5 minutes
Cook Time: 16 minutes

Country Chicken Dinner

¼ cup milk

2 tablespoons margarine or butter

1 package (4.7 ounces) PASTA RONI® Chicken & Broccoli Flavor with Linguine

2 cups frozen mixed broccoli, cauliflower and carrots vegetable medley

2 cups chopped cooked chicken or turkey

1 teaspoon dried basil leaves

1. In round 3-quart microwavable glass casserole, combine 1¾ cups water, milk and margarine. Microwave, uncovered, at HIGH 4 to 5 minutes or until boiling.

2. Gradually add pasta while stirring.

3. Stir in Special Seasonings, frozen vegetables, chicken and basil.

4. Microwave, uncovered, at HIGH 14 to 15 minutes, stirring gently after 7 minutes. Sauce will be thin, but will thicken upon standing.

5. Let stand 4 to 5 minutes or until desired consistency. Stir before serving.

Makes 4 servings

Country French Chicken Skillet

Crispy Onion Chicken Fingers

1⅓ cups *French's*® French Fried Onions

1 pound boneless skinless chicken fingers

3 to 4 tablespoons *French's*® Sweet & Tangy Honey Mustard

1. Preheat oven to 400°F. Place French Fried Onions in resealable plastic food storage bag; seal. Crush onions with rolling pin.

2. Coat chicken fingers with mustard. Dip into crushed onions. Place chicken on baking sheet.

3. Bake 15 minutes or until chicken is crispy and no longer pink in center.

Makes 4 servings

Prep Time: 10 minutes
Cook Time: 15 minutes

Quick Tip

If you can't find chicken fingers, also called chicken tenders, in your supermarket, cut boneless skinless chicken breasts lengthwise in half or in thirds.

Turkey Parmesan

⅔ cup milk

2 tablespoons margarine or butter

2 cups zucchini slices, halved

1 package (5.1 ounces) PASTA RONI® Angel Hair Pasta with Parmesan Cheese

2 cups cooked turkey strips

1 jar (2 ounces) chopped pimentos, drained

2 tablespoons grated Parmesan cheese

Microwave Directions

1. In round 3-quart microwavable glass casserole, combine 1½ cups water, milk, margarine and zucchini. Microwave, uncovered, on HIGH 6 minutes.

2. Stir in pasta, Special Seasonings and turkey. Separate pasta with fork, if needed.

3. Microwave, uncovered, on HIGH 7 to 8 minutes, stirring after 2 minutes. Separate pasta with fork, if needed.

4. Sauce will be very thin, but will thicken upon standing. Stir in pimentos and cheese.

5. Let stand 3 to 4 minutes or until desired consistency. Stir before serving.

Makes 4 servings

Crispy Onion Chicken Fingers

Yummy Weeknight Chicken

1 pound boneless skinless chicken breasts, pounded thin

1 small onion, sliced

1 package (10 ounces) mushrooms, sliced

⅓ cup barbecue sauce

¼ cup honey

2 tablespoons *French's*® Worcestershire Sauce

1. Heat *1 tablespoon oil* in large nonstick skillet over medium-high heat. Cook chicken 5 minutes until chicken is no longer pink in center. Remove chicken to serving platter; keep warm.

2. In same skillet, sauté onion and mushrooms for 5 minutes or until mushrooms are golden brown and no liquid remains. Return chicken to skillet.

3. Combine remaining ingredients. Pour into skillet. Bring to a full boil. Reduce heat and cook 2 to 3 minutes or until sauce thickens slightly, stirring occasionally. Serve with hot cooked rice, if desired.   *Makes 4 servings*

Prep Time: 10 minutes
Cook Time: 12 minutes

Lemon Garlic Chicken

4 boneless, skinless chicken breast halves (about 1¼ pounds)

¼ cup flour

2 tablespoons margarine or butter

1 envelope LIPTON® RECIPE SECRETS® Savory Herb with Garlic Soup Mix

1¾ cups water

2 tablespoons lemon juice

1. Dip chicken in flour, shaking off excess. In 12-inch nonstick skillet, melt margarine over medium-high heat; add chicken and brown 4 minutes, turning once.

2. Stir in soup mix blended with water and lemon juice.

3. Reduce heat to low and simmer covered 5 minutes or until sauce is slightly thickened and chicken is thoroughly cooked. Serve, if desired, with hot cooked rice.

Makes 4 servings

Prep Time: 5 minutes
Cook Time: 15 minutes

Yummy Weeknight Chicken

Oriental Chicken & Rice

1 (6.9-ounce) package RICE-A-RONI® Chicken Flavor

2 tablespoons margarine or butter

1 pound boneless, skinless chicken breasts, cut into thin strips

¼ cup teriyaki sauce

½ teaspoon ground ginger

1 (16-ounce) package frozen Oriental-style mixed vegetables

1. In large skillet over medium heat, sauté rice-vermicelli mix with margarine until vermicelli is golden brown.

2. Slowly stir in 2 cups water, chicken, teriyaki sauce, ginger and Special Seasonings; bring to a boil. Reduce heat to low. Cover; simmer 10 minutes.

3. Stir in vegetables. Cover; simmer 5 to 10 minutes or until rice is tender and chicken is no longer pink inside. Let stand 3 minutes.

Makes 4 servings

Variation: Use pork instead of chicken and substitute ¼ cup orange juice for ¼ cup of the water.

Prep Time: 5 minutes
Cook Time: 25 minutes

Crispy Parmesan Chicken

3 cups *French's®* French Fried Onions

½ cup mayonnaise

¼ cup *French's®* Napa Valley style Dijon Mustard

¼ cup grated Parmesan cheese

6 boneless skinless chicken breast halves (about 2 pounds)

Garnish: parsley sprigs (optional)

1. Preheat oven to 350°F. Place French Fried Onions in plastic food storage bag; crush lightly with rolling pin. Transfer to sheet of waxed paper.

2. Mix mayonnaise, mustard and Parmesan cheese in pie plate. Dip chicken into mayonnaise mixture, then into onion crumbs, pressing gently to coat well.

3. Place chicken into foil-lined 15×10-inch baking dish. Bake 25 minutes or until chicken is no longer pink in center. Garnish with parsley, if desired.

Makes 6 servings

Prep Time: 10 minutes
Cook Time: 25 minutes

Oriental Chicken & Rice

Mediterranean Shrimp & Vegetable Linguine

1 pound uncooked medium shrimp, peeled and deveined

3 teaspoons BERTOLLI® Olive Oil, divided

1 medium onion, finely chopped

1 large carrot, finely chopped

1 jar (1 pound 10 ounces) RAGÚ® Light Pasta Sauce

1 box (16 ounces) linguine, cooked and drained

1. Season shrimp, if desired, with salt and ground black pepper. In 12-inch skillet, heat 2 teaspoons oil over medium-high heat and cook shrimp, stirring occasionally, 3 minutes or until almost pink. Remove shrimp and set aside.

2. In same skillet, heat remaining 1 teaspoon oil over medium-high heat and cook onion and carrot, stirring occasionally, 5 minutes or until vegetables are tender.

3. Stir in Ragú Pasta Sauce and bring to a boil over high heat. Reduce heat to low and simmer 5 minutes. Return shrimp to skillet and simmer until shrimp turn pink. Serve over hot linguine. *Makes 6 servings*

Prep Time: 15 minutes
Cook Time: 15 minutes

Tuna Mac and Cheese

1 package (7¼ ounces) macaroni and cheese dinner

1 (7-ounce) pouch of STARKIST® Premium Albacore or Chunk Light Tuna

1 cup frozen peas

½ cup shredded Cheddar cheese

½ cup milk

1 teaspoon Italian herb seasoning

¼ teaspoon garlic powder (optional)

1 tablespoon grated Parmesan cheese

Prepare macaroni and cheese dinner according to package directions. Add remaining ingredients except Parmesan cheese. Pour into 1½-quart microwavable serving dish. Cover with vented plastic wrap; microwave on HIGH 2 minutes. Stir; continue heating on HIGH 2½ to 3½ more minutes or until cheese is melted and mixture is heated through. Sprinkle with Parmesan cheese.
Makes 5 to 6 servings

Prep Time: 20 minutes

Mediterranean Shrimp & Vegetable Linguine

Sweet & Zesty Fish with Fruit Salsa

¼ cup *French's*® Bold n' Spicy Brown Mustard

¼ cup honey

2 cups chopped assorted fresh fruit (pineapple, kiwi, strawberries and mango)

1 pound sea bass or cod fillets or other firm-fleshed white fish

1. Preheat broiler or grill. Combine mustard and honey. Stir *2 tablespoons* mustard mixture into fruit; set aside.

2. Brush remaining mustard mixture on both sides of fillets. Place in foil-lined broiler pan. Broil (or grill) fish 6 inches from heat for 8 minutes or until fish is opaque.

3. Serve fruit salsa with fish.

Makes 4 servings

Prep Time: 15 minutes
Cook Time: 8 minutes

Quick Tip

To prepare this meal even faster, purchase cut-up fresh fruit from the salad bar.

Tuna Skillet Supper

1 package (8 ounces) cream cheese, softened

1 cup milk

1 packet (1 ounce) HIDDEN VALLEY® The Original Ranch® Salad Dressing & Seasoning Mix

8 ounces uncooked spiral egg noodles

2 cups frozen petite peas, thawed

2 cans (6 ounces each) tuna or shrimp, drained

In a food processor fitted with a metal blade, blend cream cheese, milk and salad dressing & seasoning mix until smooth.

Cook pasta according to package directions; drain and combine with peas and tuna in a large skillet. Stir dressing mixture into pasta. Cook over low heat until mixture is hot.

Makes 4 to 6 servings

Original Ranch® Fish Fillets

1 packet (1 ounce) HIDDEN VALLEY® The Original Ranch® Salad Dressing & Seasoning Mix

1 package (19 ounces) breaded fish fillets or fish sticks

Shake dressing mix and fillets in large plastic bag until coated. Bake at 400°F for 23 to 25 minutes. Serve with lemon wedges.

Makes 4 to 6 servings

Twice Baked Potatoes

3 hot baked potatoes, split lengthwise

½ cup sour cream

2 tablespoons butter or margarine

1⅓ cups *French's®* French Fried Onions, divided

1 cup (4 ounces) shredded Cheddar cheese, divided

Dash paprika (optional)

1. Preheat oven to 400°F. Scoop out inside of potatoes into medium bowl, leaving thin shells. Mash potatoes with sour cream and butter until smooth. Stir in ⅔ *cup* French Fried Onions and ½ cup cheese. Spoon mixture into shells.

2. Bake 20 minutes or until heated through. Top with remaining cheese, onions and paprika, if desired. Bake 2 minutes or until cheese melts.   *Makes 6 servings*

Variation: For added Cheddar flavor, substitute *French's®* new **Cheddar French Fried Onions** for the original flavor.

Prep Time: 10 minutes
Cook Time: 22 minutes

Quick Tip

To bake potatoes quickly, microwave on HIGH (100% power)10 to 12 minutes until tender.

Hidden Valley®
Glazed Baby Carrots

¼ cup butter

¼ cup packed light brown sugar

1 package (16 ounces) ready-to-eat baby carrots, cooked

1 packet (1 ounce) HIDDEN VALLEY® The Original Ranch® Salad Dressing & Seasoning Mix

Melt butter and sugar in a large skillet. Add carrots and salad dressing & seasoning mix; stir well. Cook over medium heat until carrots are tender and glazed, about 5 minutes, stirring frequently.   *Makes 4 to 6 servings*

Garlic Fries

1 bag (32 ounces) frozen French fried potatoes

1 envelope LIPTON® RECIPE SECRETS® Savory Herb with Garlic Soup Mix*

Also terrific with LIPTON® RECIPE SECRETS® Onion Soup Mix.

1. Preheat oven to 450°F. In large bowl, thoroughly toss frozen French fried potatoes with soup mix; spread on jelly-roll pan.

2. Bake until golden and crisp, about 25 minutes, stirring once.   *Makes 4 servings*

Prep Time: 5 minutes
Cook Time: 25 minutes

Twice Baked Potatoes

Honey Mustard-Orange Roasted Vegetables

6 cups assorted cut-up vegetables (red or green bell peppers, zucchini, red onions and carrots)

2 tablespoons olive oil

1 teaspoon minced garlic

¼ cup *French's*® Sweet & Tangy Honey Mustard

2 tablespoons orange juice

1 teaspoon grated orange peel

1. Preheat oven to 450°F. Toss vegetables with oil, garlic and *1 teaspoon salt* in roasting pan.

2. Bake, uncovered, 20 minutes or until tender.

3. Toss vegetables with mustard, juice and orange peel just before serving. Serve over pasta or with bread, if desired.

Makes 6 servings

Prep Time: 10 minutes
Cook Time: 20 minutes

Zesty Corn Sauté

½ cup finely chopped onion

½ cup finely chopped red or green bell pepper

1 bag (16 ounces) frozen sweet corn

1 tablespoon *Frank's*® *RedHot*® Cayenne Pepper Sauce

1 teaspoon chili powder

1. Heat *2 tablespoons oil* in 12-inch nonstick skillet over medium-high heat. Cook onion and pepper 4 minutes or until tender, stirring occasionally.

2. Stir in corn, ***Frank's RedHot*** Sauce and chili powder. Simmer over medium heat 3 minutes or until corn is heated through. Garnish, if desired, with chopped green onion. Splash on more ***Frank's RedHot*** Sauce to taste.

Makes 4 to 6 servings

Prep Time: 5 minutes
Cook Time: 7 minutes

Quick Tip

Use the following equivalents when purchasing vegetables. One large bell pepper equals approximately 1 cup chopped pepper. 3 medium zucchini (1 pound) equal 2½ cups cubed zucchini. 4 medium onions (1 pound) equal 2 to 3 cups chopped onion.

Honey Mustard-Orange Roasted Vegetables

Savory Skillet Broccoli

1 tablespoon BERTOLLI® Olive Oil

6 cups fresh broccoli florets *or* 1 pound green beans, trimmed

1 envelope LIPTON® RECIPE SECRETS® Golden Onion Soup Mix*

1½ cups water

*Also terrific with LIPTON® RECIPE SECRETS® Onion-Mushroom Soup Mix.

1. In 12-inch skillet, heat oil over medium-high heat and cook broccoli, stirring occasionally, 2 minutes.

2. Stir in soup mix blended with water. Bring to a boil over high heat.

3. Reduce heat to medium-low and simmer, covered, 6 minutes or until broccoli is tender.

Makes 4 servings

Prep Time: 5 minutes
Cook Time: 10 minutes

Spinach Mediterranean Style

1 pound fresh spinach, washed, drained and stems removed

2 tablespoons FILIPPO BERIO® Olive Oil

1 clove garlic, minced

1 teaspoon balsamic or wine vinegar

Microwave Directions

Place spinach in microwave-safe 8- or 9-inch square baking dish. Drizzle with olive oil; sprinkle with garlic. Cover with vented plastic wrap. Microwave on HIGH (100% power) 5 minutes or until spinach is wilted, stirring halfway through cooking. Sprinkle with vinegar. *Makes 3 to 4 servings*

Baked Squash

2 medium-sized acorn squash

2 tart red apples, diced

½ cup chopped nuts

½ cup SMUCKER'S® Apple Jelly

¼ cup butter or margarine, softened

Cut squash in half crosswise or lengthwise; scoop out centers. Place in baking pan. Combine apples, nuts, jelly and butter. Fill squash with mixture. Pour a small amount of boiling water in bottom of pan around squash. Cover pan with foil.

Bake at 400°F for 45 to 60 minutes or until fork-tender. Remove foil during last 5 minutes of baking. *Makes 4 servings*

Savory Skillet Broccoli

Buffalo Chili Onions

½ cup *Frank's® RedHot®* Cayenne Pepper Sauce

½ cup (1 stick) butter or margarine, melted or olive oil

¼ cup chili sauce

1 tablespoon chili powder

4 large sweet onions, cut into ½-inch-thick slices

Whisk together *Frank's RedHot* Sauce, butter, chili sauce and chili powder in medium bowl until blended; brush on onion slices.

Place onions on grid. Grill over medium-high coals 10 minutes or until tender, turning and basting often with the chili mixture. Serve warm.   *Makes 6 side-dish servings*

Tip: Onions may be prepared ahead and grilled just before serving.

Prep Time: 10 minutes
Cook Time: 10 minutes

Cheddar Broccoli Potatoes

6 hot baked potatoes, split open lengthwise

1½ cups chopped, cooked broccoli

1⅓ cups *French's®* French Fried Onions

¾ cup pasteurized process American cheese sauce, melted

1. Place potatoes on microwave-safe dish. Scrape cooked potato with fork to fluff up. Top with broccoli and French Fried Onions, dividing evenly.

2. Microwave on HIGH 2 minutes or until onions are golden.

3. Drizzle melted cheese sauce on top.
Makes 6 servings

Prep Time: 20 minutes
Cook Time: 2 minutes

Hidden Valley® Red Pepper Pasta

1 packet (1 ounce) HIDDEN VALLEY® The Original Ranch® Salad Dressing & Seasoning Mix

1 cup milk

1 cup mayonnaise

2 packages (9 ounces *each*) fresh spinach tortellini, cooked and drained

1 jar (7.25 ounces) roasted red peppers, rinsed, drained and cut into strips

½ teaspoon dried, chopped basil leaves

In bowl, prepare dressing by combining milk and mayonnaise with dressing mix. Mix well. Cover and refrigerate. Chill 30 minutes to thicken. Stir together 1 cup prepared dressing, tortellini, peppers and basil in large saucepan. Heat thoroughly. (Refrigerate remaining 1 cup prepared dressing for later use.)
Makes 4 to 6 servings

Buffalo Chili Onions

Rush Hour Dinners

Make-Ahead Desserts

No-Bake Chocolate Peanut Butter Bars

2 cups peanut butter, *divided*
¾ cup (1½ sticks) butter, softened
2 cups powdered sugar, *divided*
3 cups graham cracker crumbs
2 cups (12-ounce package) NESTLÉ® TOLL HOUSE® Semi-Sweet
  Chocolate Mini Morsels, *divided*

GREASE 13×9-inch baking pan.

BEAT 1¼ cups peanut butter and butter in large mixer bowl until creamy. Gradually beat in *1 cup* powdered sugar. With hands or wooden spoon, work in *remaining* powdered sugar, graham cracker crumbs and ½ *cup* morsels. Press evenly into prepared pan. Smooth top with spatula.

MELT *remaining* peanut butter and *remaining* morsels in medium, *heavy-duty* saucepan over *lowest possible heat,* stirring constantly, until smooth. Spread over graham cracker crust in pan. Refrigerate for at least 1 hour or until chocolate is firm; cut into bars. Store in refrigerator.   *Makes 5 dozen bars*

Cherry Cupcakes

1 (18¾-ounce) box chocolate cake mix

3 eggs

1⅓ cups water

½ cup vegetable oil

1 (21-ounce) can cherry pie filling

1 (16-ounce) can vanilla frosting

Prepare cake mix according to package directions, adding eggs, water and oil. Pour batter into 24 paper-lined muffin-pan cups, filling two-thirds full.

Remove 24 cherries from cherry filling; set aside. Spoon a generous teaspoon of remaining cherry filling onto the center of each cupcake.

Bake in preheated 350°F oven 20 to 25 minutes. Cool in pans on wire racks 10 minutes. Remove from pan. Let cool completely. Frost cupcakes with vanilla frosting. Garnish cupcakes with reserved cherries. *Makes 24 cupcakes*

Favorite recipe from **Cherry Marketing Institute**

Blueberry Cheesecake

1 (8-ounce) package cream cheese, softened

½ cup sugar

2 eggs, beaten

1 (6-ounce) READY CRUST® Graham Cracker Pie Crust

1 (21-ounce) can blueberry pie filling

Frozen whipped topping, thawed

1. Preheat oven to 325°F. Beat cream cheese, sugar and eggs in small bowl until fluffy. Place crust on baking sheet. Pour mixture into crust.

2. Bake 25 to 30 minutes or until center is almost set. Cool.

3. Spread blueberry filing on top. Garnish with whipped topping. Chill 3 hours. Refrigerate leftovers. *Makes 8 servings*

Prep Time: 10 minutes
Bake Time: 25 to 30 minutes
Chill Time: 3 hours

Cherry Cupcakes

Make-Ahead Desserts

Double Nut Chocolate Chip Cookies

1 package DUNCAN HINES® Moist Deluxe® Classic Yellow Cake Mix

½ cup butter or margarine, melted

1 egg

1 cup semisweet chocolate chips

½ cup finely chopped pecans

1 cup sliced almonds, divided

1. Preheat oven to 375°F. Grease baking sheets.

2. Combine cake mix, butter and egg in large bowl. Mix at low speed with electric mixer until just blended. Stir in chocolate chips, pecans and ¼ cup almonds. Shape rounded tablespoonfuls of dough into balls. Place remaining ¾ cup almonds in shallow bowl. Press tops of cookies into almonds. Place 1 inch apart on prepared baking sheets.

3. Bake at 375°F for 9 to 11 minutes or until lightly browned. Cool 2 minutes on baking sheets. Remove to cooling racks.

Makes 3 to 3½ dozen cookies

Fudgy Peanut Butter Cake

1 (18.25-ounce) box chocolate fudge cake mix

2 eggs

1½ cups plus ⅔ cup water, divided

1 (16-ounce) package chocolate fudge frosting mix

1¼ cups SMUCKER'S® Chunky Natural Peanut Butter

Grease and flour 10-inch tube pan. In large bowl, blend cake mix, eggs and 1½ cups water until moistened; mix as directed on cake package. Pour batter into pan.

In medium bowl, combine frosting mix, peanut butter and ⅔ cup water; blend until smooth. Spoon over batter in pan.

Bake in preheated 350°F oven 35 to 45 minutes or until top springs back when touched lightly in center. Cool upright in pan 1 hour; remove from pan. Cool completely.

Makes 12 to 15 servings

Quick Tip

If you have leftover cookies and cake, divide into individual portions and wrap tightly in plastic wrap. You'll have the perfect treat ready for a lunch box, brown bag meal or late night snack.

Double Nut Chocolate Chip Cookies

Make-Ahead Desserts

Funky Devil's Fudge Sauce

1 can (14 ounces) sweetened condensed milk (not evaporated milk)

1 package (12 ounces) semi-sweet chocolate chips

¼ cup whole milk

3 tablespoons *Frank's® RedHot®* Cayenne Pepper Sauce

Ice cream or pound cake (optional)

Combine condensed milk, chocolate and whole milk in large microwavable bowl. Microwave at HIGH 3 minutes or until chocolate is melted, stirring once. Add ***Frank's RedHot*** Sauce; stir until smooth. Serve over ice cream or cake, if desired. Garnish as desired. Refrigerate any leftover sauce.*   *Makes 2½ cups*

*Leftover sauce may be reheated in microwave. Microwave and stir for 30 seconds at a time. If sauce becomes too thick, just stir in small amount of whole milk.

Serving Suggestion: This sauce is also great as a fondue dipping sauce. Serve with cubed pound cake, fresh strawberries, oranges segments, apple wedges, sliced peeled kiwifruit and cubed fresh pineapple.

Prep Time: 5 minutes
Cook Time: 3 minutes

Peanut Butter "Makes Everything Better" Bars

1¼ cups "M&M's"® Milk Chocolate Mini Baking Bits, divided

1 package (18 ounces) refrigerated sugar cookie dough

½ cup creamy peanut butter

¼ cup all-purpose flour

¼ cup powdered sugar

1 square (1 ounce) milk chocolate

Preheat oven to 350°F. Lightly grease 8×8×2-inch baking pan; set aside. In medium bowl stir 1 cup "M&M's"® Milk Chocolate Mini Baking Bits into dough. In small bowl beat peanut butter, flour and powdered sugar until well combined. Reserve ½ of cookie dough. Press remaining dough into prepared pan; layer with peanut butter mixture. Top with reserved dough. Bake 20 to 25 minutes or until golden brown. Remove pan to wire rack; cool completely. Place chocolate square in small microwave-safe bowl. Microwave at HIGH 20 seconds; stir. Repeat as necessary until chocolate is completely melted, stirring at 10-second intervals. Drizzle melted chocolate over bars and sprinkle with remaining ¼ cup "M&M's"® Milk Chocolate Mini Baking Bits. Cut into bars. Store in tightly covered container.   *Makes 16 bars*

Funky Devil's Fudge Sauce

Granola Bars

3 cups oats

1 (14-ounce) can EAGLE® BRAND
  Sweetened Condensed Milk
  (NOT evaporated milk)

1 cup peanuts

1 cup sunflower seeds

1 cup raisins

½ cup (1 stick) butter or margarine, melted

1½ teaspoons ground cinnamon

1. Preheat oven to 325°F. Line 15×10-inch jelly-roll pan with aluminum foil; grease.

2. In large mixing bowl, combine all ingredients; mix well. Press evenly into prepared pan.

3. Bake 25 to 30 minutes or until golden brown. Cool slightly; remove from pan and peel off foil. Cut into bars. Store loosely covered at room temperature.

Makes 48 bars

Prep Time: 20 minutes
Bake Time: 25 to 30 minutes

Chocolate Ice Cream Cups

1 (12-ounce) package semi-sweet
  chocolate chips (2 cups)

1 (14-ounce) can EAGLE® BRAND
  Sweetened Condensed Milk
  (NOT evaporated milk)

1 cup finely ground pecans

  Ice cream, any flavor

1. In heavy saucepan over low heat, melt chips with Eagle Brand; remove from heat. Stir in pecans. In individual paper-lined muffin cups, spread about 2 tablespoons chocolate mixture. With lightly greased spoon, spread chocolate on bottom and up side of each cup.

2. Freeze 2 hours or until firm. Before serving, remove paper liners. Fill chocolate cups with ice cream. Store unfilled cups tightly covered in freezer.   *Makes about 1½ dozen cups*

Note: It is easier to remove the paper liners if the chocolate cups sit at room temperature for about 5 minutes first.

Quick Tip

To trim the fat in these Eagle Brand recipes, substitute Eagle Brand Fat Free or Low Fat Sweetened Condensed Milk.

Make-Ahead Desserts

Toffee Bits Cheesecake Cups

About 16 to 18 vanilla wafer cookies

3 packages (8 ounces each) cream cheese, softened

¾ cup sugar

3 eggs

1 teaspoon vanilla extract

1¼ cups SKOR® English Toffee Bits or HEATH® BITS 'O BRICKLE™ Almond Toffee Bits, divided

1. Heat oven to 350°F. Line 2½-inch muffin cups with paper bake cups; place vanilla wafer on bottom of each cup.

2. Beat cream cheese and sugar in large bowl on low speed of mixer until smooth. Beat in eggs and vanilla just until blended. Do not overbeat. Set aside ¼ cup toffee bits. Gently stir remaining 1 cup bits into batter; pour into prepared cups to ¼ inch from top.

3. Bake 20 to 25 minutes or until almost set. Remove from oven. Immediately sprinkle about ½ teaspoon toffee bits onto each cup. Cool completely in pan on wire rack. Remove from pan. Cover; refrigerate about 3 hours. Store leftover cups in refrigerator.

Makes about 16 to 18 cups

Chocolate Peanut Butter Pie

1 (14-ounce) can chocolate sweetened condensed milk

¼ cup creamy peanut butter

1 (8-ounce) tub frozen non-dairy whipped topping, thawed

1 (6-ounce) READY CRUST® Graham Cracker Pie Crust

1. Combine sweetened condensed milk and peanut butter in large bowl; mix well. Fold in whipped topping. Spoon into crust.

2. Freeze 6 hours. Garnish as desired. Freeze leftovers. *Makes 8 servings*

Prep Time: 5 minutes
Freeze Time: 6 hours

Quick Tip

Chocolate curls are a beautiful finishing touch for the top of a delicious dessert. Place a 1-ounce square of chocolate on a small microwavable plate and heat at HIGH (100%) 5 to 10 seconds. (Chocolate should still be firm.) Pull a vegetable peeler across the chocolate to create curls. Place the curls on a waxed paper-lined baking sheet and refrigerate 15 minutes or until firm.

Toffee Bits Cheesecake Cups

Make-Ahead Desserts

Scrumptious Minted Brownies

1 (21-ounce) package DUNCAN HINES®
    Family-Style Chewy Fudge
    Brownie Mix
1 egg
⅓ cup water
⅓ cup vegetable oil
48 chocolate crème de menthe candy
    wafers, divided

1. Preheat oven to 350°F. Grease bottom only of 13×9-inch pan.

2. Combine brownie mix, egg, water and oil in large bowl. Stir with spoon until well blended, about 50 strokes. Spread in prepared pan. Bake at 350°F for 25 minutes or until set. Place 30 candy wafers evenly over hot brownies. Let stand for 1 minute to melt. Spread candy wafers to frost brownies. Score frosting into 36 bars by running tip of knife through melted candy. (Do not cut through brownies.) Cut remaining 18 candy wafers in half lengthwise; place halves on each scored bar. Cool completely. Cut into bars.

Makes 36 brownies

Microwave Double Peanut Bars

½ cup light brown sugar
½ cup light corn syrup or honey
½ cup creamy peanut butter
6 shredded wheat biscuits, coarsely
    crushed
¾ cup raisins
½ cup chopped peanuts

In 2-quart microwavable bowl, blend sugar, corn syrup and peanut butter. Microwave on HIGH(100% power) 1 to 1½ minutes until bubbly. Stir until smooth. Quickly stir in cereal, raisins and peanuts. Press evenly into greased 8- or 9-inch square baking pan. Cool. Cut into bars.

Makes 2 dozen bars

Favorite recipe from **Peanut Advisory Board**

Quick Tip

For an easy glaze, sprinkle bar cookies with chocolate chips immediately after baking, then cover with foil. After 3 to 4 minutes, remove the foil and spread the melted chips over the bars.

Scrumptious Minted Brownies

Make-Ahead Desserts

Lemony Cheesecake Bars

1½ cups graham cracker crumbs

⅓ cup sugar

⅓ cup finely chopped pecans

⅓ cup butter or margarine, melted

2 (8-ounce) packages cream cheese, softened

1 (14-ounce) can EAGLE® BRAND Sweetened Condensed Milk (NOT evaporated milk)

2 eggs

½ cup lemon juice from concentrate

1. Preheat oven to 325°F. In medium mixing bowl, combine crumbs, sugar, pecans and melted butter. Reserve ⅓ cup crumb mixture; press remaining mixture firmly on bottom of ungreased 13×9-inch baking pan. Bake 5 minutes. Remove from oven and cool on wire rack.

2. In large mixing bowl, beat cream cheese until fluffy. Gradually beat in Eagle Brand until smooth. Add eggs; beat until just combined. Stir in lemon juice. Carefully spoon mixture onto crust in pan. Spoon reserved crumb mixture to make diagonal stripes on top of cheese mixture or sprinkle to cover.

3. Bake about 30 minutes or until knife inserted near center comes out clean. Cool on wire rack 1 hour. Cut into bars to serve. Store covered in refrigerator.   *Makes 3 dozen bars*

Prep Time: 25 minutes
Bake Time: 35 minutes

Crispy Cocoa Bars

¼ cup (½ stick) margarine

¼ cup HERSHEY'S Cocoa

5 cups miniature marshmallows

5 cups crisp rice cereal

1. Spray 13×9×2-inch pan with vegetable cooking spray.

2. Melt margarine in large saucepan over low heat; stir in cocoa and marshmallows. Cook over low heat, stirring constantly, until marshmallows are melted and mixture is smooth and well blended. Continue cooking 1 minute, stirring constantly. Remove from heat.

3. Add cereal; stir until coated. Lightly spray spatula with vegetable cooking spray; press mixture into prepared pan. Cool completely. Cut into bars.   *Makes 24 bars*

Quick Tip

Cut bars on the diagonal to make festive-shaped triangles or diamonds. For kid's parties, cut out the cookies with cookie cutters.

Lemony Cheesecake Bars

Heavenly Chocolate Mousse Pie

4 (1-ounce) squares unsweetened chocolate, melted
1 (14-ounce) can EAGLE® BRAND Sweetened Condensed Milk (NOT evaporated milk)
1½ teaspoons vanilla extract
1 cup (½ pint) whipping cream, whipped
1 (6-ounce) chocolate crumb pie crust

1. In medium mixing bowl, beat melted chocolate with Eagle Brand and vanilla until well blended.

2. Chill 15 minutes or until cooled; stir until smooth. Fold in whipped cream.

3. Pour into crust. Chill thoroughly. Garnish as desired. Refrigerate leftovers.   *Makes 1 pie*

Prep Time: 20 minutes
Chill Time: 15 minutes

Quick Tip

Depending on the occasion, garnish this pie with a dollop of whipped cream, then sprinkle with a dash of cinnamon, colored sprinkles, crushed hard peppermint candy, chocolate curls, sliced fresh strawberries or raspberries.

Mocha Truffles

¼ cup whipping cream
3 tablespoons sugar
3 tablespoons butter
1½ teaspoons powdered instant coffee
½ cup HERSHEY'S Semi-Sweet Chocolate Chips
½ teaspoon vanilla extract
Chopped nuts or HERSHEY'S Semi-Sweet Baking Chocolate, grated

1. Combine whipping cream, sugar, butter and instant coffee in small saucepan. Cook over low heat, stirring constantly, just until mixture boils.

2. Remove from heat; immediately add chocolate chips. Stir until chips are melted and mixture is smooth when stirred; add vanilla. Pour into small bowl; refrigerate, stirring occasionally, until mixture begins to set. Cover; refrigerate several hours or overnight to allow mixture to ripen and harden.

3. Shape small amounts of mixture into 1-inch balls, working quickly to prevent melting; roll in nuts or chocolate. Cover; store in refrigerator. Serve cold.
Makes about 16 truffles

Make-Ahead Desserts

Peppermint Chocolate Fudge

1 (12-ounce) package milk chocolate chips (2 cups)

1 cup (6 ounces) semi-sweet chocolate chips

1 (14-ounce) can EAGLE® BRAND Sweetened Condensed Milk (NOT evaporated milk)

Dash salt

½ teaspoon peppermint extract

¼ cup crushed hard peppermint candy

1. In heavy saucepan over low heat, melt chips with Eagle Brand and salt. Remove from heat; stir in peppermint extract. Spread evenly in foil-lined 8- or 9-inch square pan. Sprinkle with peppermint candy.

2. Chill 2 hours or until firm. Turn fudge onto cutting board; peel off foil and cut into squares. Store loosely covered at room temperature.   *Makes about 2 pounds fudge*

Prep Time: 10 minutes
Chill Time: 2 hours

Dipped Fruit

2 cups (12-ounces package) NESTLÉ® TOLL HOUSE® Semi-Sweet Chocolate Morsels or NESTLÉ® TOLL HOUSE® Premier White Morsels

2 tablespoons vegetable shortening

24 bite-size pieces fresh fruit (strawberries, orange, kiwi, banana or melon), rinsed and patted dry

LINE baking sheet with wax paper.

MICROWAVE morsels and shortening in medium, microwave-safe bowl on MEDIUM-HIGH (70%) power for 1 minute; stir. Microwave at additional 10- to 20-second intervals, stirring until smooth.

DIP fruit into melted morsels; shake off excess. Place on prepared baking sheet; refrigerate until set.   *Makes about 2 dozen pieces*

For a fancy drizzle: MICROWAVE ½ cup NESTLÉ® TOLL HOUSE® Semi-Sweet Chocolate or Premier White Morsels or Baking Bars, broken in pieces, in small, *heavy-duty* resealable plastic food storage bag on MEDIUM-HIGH (70%) power for 1 minute; knead. Microwave at additional 10- to 20-second intervals, kneading until smooth. Cut tiny corner from bag; squeeze to drizzle over fruit. Refrigerate until set.

Peppermint Chocolate Fudge

Make-Ahead Desserts

Sweet Walnut Maple Bars

Crust

1 package DUNCAN HINES® Moist Deluxe® Classic Yellow Cake Mix, divided

⅓ cup butter or margarine, melted

1 egg

Topping

1⅓ cups MRS. BUTTERWORTH'S® Maple Syrup

3 eggs

⅓ cup firmly packed light brown sugar

½ teaspoon maple flavoring or vanilla extract

1 cup chopped walnuts

1. Preheat oven to 350°F. Grease 13×9×2-inch pan.

2. For crust, reserve ⅔ cup cake mix; set aside. Combine remaining cake mix, melted butter and egg in large bowl. Stir until thoroughly blended. (Mixture will be crumbly.) Press into prepared pan. Bake at 350°F for 15 to 20 minutes or until light golden brown.

3. For topping, combine reserved cake mix, maple syrup, eggs, brown sugar and maple flavoring in large bowl. Beat at low speed with electric mixer for 3 minutes. Pour over crust. Sprinkle with walnuts. Bake at 350°F for 30 to 35 minutes or until filling is set. Cool completely. Cut into bars. Store leftover cookie bars in refrigerator. *Makes 24 bars*

Cherry Dream

5 cups loosely packed angel food cake cubes (about 10 ounces) *or* ½ of large angel food cake

1 (21-ounce) can cherry pie filling

1¾ cups (4 ounces) frozen non-dairy whipped topping, thawed

Fresh mint, for garnish

Sprinkle cake cubes in bottom of 9-inch square baking pan. Fold cherry pie filling into whipped topping in medium bowl. Spoon cherry mixture evenly over cake cubes. Let chill, covered, several hours or overnight. Garnish each serving with sprig of mint.

Makes 8 servings

Favorite recipe from **Cherry Marketing Institute**

Quick Tip

Cherry Dream is a great dessert for a potluck. Make this dessert in a decorative serving dish or pan. Garnish and you'll have an easy delicious dessert.

Make-Ahead Desserts

Upside-Down German Chocolate Cake

1½ cups flaked coconut

1½ cups chopped pecans

1 package DUNCAN HINES® Moist Deluxe® German Chocolate or Classic Chocolate Cake Mix

1 package (8 ounces) cream cheese, softened

½ cup butter or margarine, melted

1 pound (3½ to 4 cups) confectioners' sugar

1. Preheat oven to 350°F. Grease and flour 13×9-inch pan.

2. Spread coconut evenly on bottom of prepared pan. Sprinkle with pecans. Prepare cake mix as directed on package. Pour over coconut and pecans. Combine cream cheese and melted butter in medium mixing bowl. Beat at low speed with electric mixer until creamy. Add sugar; beat until blended and smooth. Drop by spoonfuls evenly over cake batter. Bake at 350°F for 45 to 50 minutes or until toothpick inserted halfway to bottom of cake comes out clean. Cool completely in pan. To serve, cut into individual pieces; turn upside down onto plate.

Makes 12 to 16 servings

Macaroon Kisses

1 (14-ounce) can EAGLE® BRAND Sweetened Condensed Milk (NOT evaporated milk)

2 teaspoons vanilla extract

1 to 1½ teaspoons almond extract

5⅓ cups (14 ounces) flaked coconut

48 solid milk chocolate candy kisses, stars or drops, unwrapped

1. Preheat oven to 325°F. Line baking sheets with foil; grease and flour foil. Set aside.

2. In large mixing bowl, combine Eagle Brand, vanilla and almond extract. Stir in coconut. Drop by rounded teaspoonfuls onto prepared baking sheets; with spoon slightly flatten each mound.

3. Bake 15 to 17 minutes or until golden brown. Remove from oven. Immediately press candy kiss, star or drop in center of each macaroon. Remove from baking sheets; cool on wire racks. Store loosely covered at room temperature. *Makes 4 dozen cookies*

Quick Tip

Store leftover coconut in the refrigerator and use within four weeks.

Upside-Down German Chocolate Cake

Brownie Gems

1 package DUNCAN HINES® Chocolate Lover's® Double Fudge Brownie Mix

2 eggs

2 tablespoons water

⅓ cup vegetable oil

28 miniature peanut butter cup or chocolate kiss candies

1 container of your favorite Duncan Hines frosting

1. Preheat oven to 350°F. Spray (1¾-inch) mini-muffin pans with vegetable cooking spray or line with foil baking cups.

2. Combine brownie mix, fudge packet from mix, eggs, water and oil in large bowl. Stir with spoon until well blended, about 50 strokes. Drop 1 heaping teaspoonful of batter into each muffin cup; top with candy. Cover candy with more batter. Bake at 350°F for 15 to 17 minutes.

3. Cool 5 minutes. Carefully loosen brownies from pan. Remove to cool completely. Frost and decorate as desired.

Makes 30 brownie gems

Cherries in the Snow Dessert

1 package DUNCAN HINES® Angel Food Cake Mix

1 package (8 ounces) cream cheese, softened

1 cup confectioners' sugar

1 container (12 ounces) frozen whipped topping, thawed

1 can (21 ounces) cherry pie filling

1. Preheat oven to 375°F. Prepare, bake and cool cake following package directions. Cut cake into 16 slices.

2. Combine cream cheese and confectioners' sugar in small bowl. Beat at medium speed with electric mixer until smooth.

3. To assemble, spread half the whipped topping in bottom of 13×9×2-inch pan. Arrange 8 cake slices on whipped topping; press lightly. Spread with cream cheese mixture. Arrange remaining cake slices on cream cheese mixture; press lightly. Spread with remaining whipped topping. Spoon cherry pie filling evenly over top. (Pan will be filled to the brim.) Refrigerate for 2 hours or until ready to serve. Cut into squares.

Makes 16 to 20 servings

Brownie Gems

Make-Ahead Desserts

Marshmallow Krispie Bars

1 (21-ounce) package DUNCAN HINES®
    Family-Style Chewy Fudge
    Brownie Mix
1 package (10½ ounces) miniature
    marshmallows
1½ cups semisweet chocolate chips
1 cup creamy peanut butter
1 tablespoon butter or margarine
1½ cups crisp rice cereal

1. Preheat oven to 350°F. Grease bottom only of 13×9-inch pan.

2. Prepare and bake brownies following package directions for cake-like recipe. Remove from oven. Sprinkle marshmallows on hot brownies. Return to oven. Bake for 3 minutes longer.

3. Place chocolate chips, peanut butter and butter in medium saucepan. Cook over low heat, stirring constantly, until chips are melted. Add rice cereal; mix well. Spread mixture over marshmallow layer. Refrigerate until chilled. Cut into bars.

Makes about 2 dozen bars

Quick Tip

For a special presentation, cut bars into diamond shapes.

Pumpkin Cheesecake Bars

1 (16-ounce) package pound cake mix
3 eggs, divided
2 tablespoons butter or margarine, melted
4 teaspoons pumpkin pie spice, divided
1 (8-ounce) package cream cheese,
    softened
1 (14-ounce) can EAGLE® BRAND
    Sweetened Condensed Milk
    (NOT evaporated milk)
1 (15-ounce) can pumpkin
½ teaspoon salt
1 cup chopped nuts

1. Preheat oven to 350°F. In large mixing bowl, beat cake mix, 1 egg, butter and 2 teaspoons pumpkin pie spice on low speed of electric mixer until crumbly. Press onto bottom of ungreased 15×10×1-inch jelly-roll pan.

2. In large mixing bowl, beat cream cheese until fluffy. Gradually beat in Eagle Brand until smooth. Beat in remaining 2 eggs, pumpkin, remaining 2 teaspoons pumpkin pie spice and salt; mix well. Pour over crust; sprinkle with nuts.

3. Bake 30 to 35 minutes or until set. Cool. Chill; cut into bars. Store covered in refrigerator.

Makes 4 dozen bars

Marshmallow Krispie Bars

Make-Ahead Desserts

White & Chocolate Covered Strawberries

1⅔ cups (10-ounce package) HERSHEY'S Premier White Chips

2 tablespoons shortening (do not use butter, margarine, spread or oil)

1 cup HERSHEY'S Semi-Sweet Chocolate Chips

4 cups (2 pints) fresh strawberries, rinsed, patted dry and chilled

1. Cover tray with wax paper.

2. Place white chips and 1 tablespoon shortening in medium microwave-safe bowl. Microwave at HIGH (100%) 1 minute; stir until chips are melted and mixture is smooth. If necessary, microwave at HIGH an additional 30 seconds at a time, just until smooth when stirred.

3. Holding by top, dip ⅔ of each strawberry into white chip mixture; shake gently to remove excess. Place on prepare tray; refrigerate until coating is firm, at least 30 minutes.

4. Repeat microwave procedure with chocolate chips in clean microwave-safe bowl. Dip lower ⅓ of each berry into chocolate mixture. Refrigerate until firm. Cover; refrigerate leftover strawberries.

Makes 2 to 3 dozen berries

No Bake Peanut Butter Pie

4 ounces cream cheese

1 cup confectioners' sugar, sifted

1 cup crunchy peanut butter

½ cup milk

8 ounces frozen whipped topping, thawed

1 deep-dish graham cracker or chocolate-flavored crust

In large mixer bowl combine cream cheese and confectioners' sugar; mix well. Add peanut butter and mix. Slowly add milk and mix well. Fold in whipped topping. Pour into pie shell and cover. Freeze for at least 30 minutes. If desired, drizzle each serving with chocolate syrup.   *Makes 1 pie*

Favorite recipe from **Peanut Advisory Board**

Quick Tip

This pie can be made ahead and stored in the freezer for one to two weeks. For easier serving, slice before freezing. Remove to the refrigerator 30 minutes to 1 hour before serving.

Carnation® Key Lime Pie

1 *prepared* 9-inch (6 ounces) graham
   cracker crumb crust

1 can (14 ounces) NESTLÉ® CARNATION®
   Sweetened Condensed Milk

½ cup (about 3 medium limes) fresh lime
   juice

1 teaspoon grated lime peel

2 cups frozen whipped topping, thawed

   Lime peel twists or lime slices (optional)

BEAT sweetened condensed milk and lime
juice in small mixer bowl until combined; stir
in lime peel. Pour into crust; spread with
whipped topping. Refrigerate for 2 hours or
until set. Garnish with lime peel twists.

Makes 8 servings

Peter Pan's Coconut Clusters

1 (8-ounce) package hard shell chocolate
   (confectionery coating)

½ cup PETER PAN® Creamy Peanut Butter

2 cups shredded coconut

¾ cups peanuts, coarsely chopped

In microwave-safe bowl, melt chocolate pieces
and Peter Pan Peanut Butter in microwave on
HIGH (100%) for 30-second intervals, until
chocolate is melted. Stir after *each* interval;
blend well. Add coconut and peanuts; stir
gently until well coated. Drop by teaspoonfuls
onto waxed paper-lined baking sheet. Let
candy clusters harden completely before
serving. *Makes 18 candy clusters*

Mini Morsel Ice Cream Pie

1½ cups graham cracker crumbs

½ cup (1 stick) butter, melted

¼ cup granulated sugar

1 cup (6 ounces) NESTLÉ® TOLL HOUSE®
   Semi-Sweet Chocolate Mini Morsels

1 quart ice cream or frozen yogurt,
   softened

COMBINE graham cracker crumbs, butter and
sugar in medium bowl; stir in morsels. Press
2½ cups crumb mixture evenly on bottom and
side of 9-inch pie plate. Freeze for 15 minutes
or until firm. Spread softened ice cream evenly
in pie shell. Top with *remaining* crumb
mixture; freeze for 2 hours or until firm.

Makes 8 servings

Quick Tip

*To easily make graham cracker crumbs, place
graham crackers into a large plastic food storage
bag and close. Roll with a rolling pin until fine
crumbs are formed.*

Make-Ahead Desserts

Feed the Kids

Hot Dog Burritos

  1 can (16 ounces) pork and beans
⅓ cup ketchup
2 tablespoons brown sugar
2 tablespoons *French's*® **Classic Yellow**® **Mustard**
8 frankfurters, cooked
8 (8-inch) flour tortillas, heated

1. Combine beans, ketchup, brown sugar and mustard in medium saucepan. Bring to a boil over medium-high heat. Reduce heat to low and simmer 2 minutes.

2. Arrange frankfurters in heated tortillas and top with bean mixture. Roll up jelly-roll style.

Makes 8 servings

Variation: Try topping dogs with *French's*® French Fried Onions before rolling up!

Prep Time: 5 minutes
Cook Time: 8 minutes

Hot Dog Burrito

Make Your Own Pizza Shapes

1 package (10 ounces) refrigerated pizza dough

¼ to ½ cup prepared pizza sauce

1 cup shredded mozzarella cheese

1 cup *French's*® French Fried Onions

1. Preheat oven to 425°F. Unroll dough onto greased baking sheet. Press or roll dough into 12×8-inch rectangle. With sharp knife or pizza cutter, cut dough into large shape of your choice (butterfly, heart, star). Reroll scraps and cut into mini shapes. (See Quick Tip.)

2. Pre-bake crust 7 minutes or until crust just begins to brown. Spread with sauce and top with cheese. Bake 6 minutes or until crust is deep golden brown.

3. Sprinkle with French Fried Onions. Bake 2 minutes longer or until golden.

Makes 4 to 6 servings

Prep Time: 10 minutes
Cook Time: 15 minutes

Quick Tip

Pizza dough can be cut with 6-inch shaped cookie cutters. Spread with sauce and top with cheese. Bake about 10 minutes or until crust is golden. Sprinkle with French Fried Onions. Bake 2 minutes longer.

Funny Face Sandwich Melts

2 super-size English muffins, split and toasted

8 teaspoons *French's*® Sweet & Tangy Honey Mustard

1 can (8 ounces) crushed pineapple, drained

8 ounces sliced smoked ham

4 slices Swiss cheese or white American cheese

1. Place English muffins, cut side up, on baking sheet. Spread each with *2 teaspoons* mustard. Arrange one-fourth of the pineapple, ham and cheese on top, dividing evenly.

2. Broil until cheese melts, about 1 minute. Decorate with mustard and assorted vegetables to create your own funny face.

Makes 4 servings

Tip: This sandwich is also easy to prepare in the toaster oven.

Prep Time: 10 minutes
Cook Time: 1 minute

Kids' Quesadillas

8 slices American cheese

8 (10-inch) flour tortillas

6 tablespoons *French's*® Sweet & Tangy Honey Mustard

½ pound thinly sliced deli turkey

2 tablespoons melted butter

¼ teaspoon paprika

1. To prepare 1 quesadilla, arrange 2 slices of cheese on 1 tortilla. Top with one-fourth of the turkey. Spread with *1½ tablespoons* mustard, then top with another tortilla. Prepare 3 more quesadillas with remaining ingredients.

2. Combine butter and paprika. Brush one side of tortilla with butter mixture. Preheat 12-inch nonstick skillet over medium-high heat. Arrange tortilla butter side down and cook 2 minutes. Brush tortilla with butter mixture and turn over. Cook 1½ minutes or until golden brown. Repeat with remaining three quesadillas.

3. Slice into wedges before serving.

Makes 4 servings

Prep Time: 5 minutes
Cook Time: 15 minutes

Tuna 'n' Celery Sticks

4 ounces cream cheese, softened

3 tablespoons plain yogurt or mayonnaise

1½ teaspoons dried basil

1 (7-ounce) pouch of STARKIST® Premium Albacore or Chunk Light Tuna

½ cup finely grated carrot or zucchini

½ cup finely shredded Cheddar cheese

2 teaspoons instant minced onion

10 to 12 celery stalks, cleaned and strings removed

In large bowl, mix together cream cheese, yogurt and basil until smooth. Add tuna, carrot, Cheddar cheese and onion; mix well. Spread mixture into celery stalks; cut into fourths.　　　　*Makes 6 to 8 servings*

Prep Time: 10 minutes

Festive Franks

1 can (8 ounces) reduced-fat crescent roll dough

5½ teaspoons barbecue sauce

⅓ cup finely shredded reduced-fat sharp Cheddar cheese

8 fat-free hot dogs

¼ teaspoon poppy seeds (optional)

Additional barbecue sauce (optional)

1. Preheat oven to 350°F. Spray large baking sheet with nonstick cooking spray; set aside.

2. Unroll dough and separate into 8 triangles. Cut each triangle in half lengthwise to make 2 triangles. Lightly spread barbecue sauce over each triangle. Sprinkle with cheese.

3. Cut each hot dog in half; trim off rounded ends. Place one hot dog piece at large end of one dough triangle. Roll up jelly-roll style from wide end. Place point-side down on prepared baking sheet. Sprinkle with poppy seeds, if desired. Repeat with remaining hot dog pieces and dough.

4. Bake 13 minutes or until dough is golden brown. Cool 1 to 2 minutes on baking sheet. Serve with additional barbecue sauce for dipping, if desired. *Makes 6 to 8 servings*

Taco Taters

1 pound ground beef

1 jar (1 pound 10 ounces) RAGÚ® Old World Style® Pasta Sauce

1 package (1.25 ounces) taco seasoning mix

6 large all-purpose potatoes, unpeeled and baked

1. In 12-inch skillet, brown ground beef over medium-high heat; drain. Stir in Ragú Pasta Sauce and taco seasoning mix and cook 5 minutes.

2. To serve, cut a lengthwise slice from top of each potato. Evenly spoon beef mixture onto each potato. Garnish, if desired, with shredded Cheddar cheese and sour cream.

Makes 6 servings

Prep Time: 5 minutes
Cook Time: 15 minutes

Quick Tip

To speed up the cooking time for baked potatoes, place the potatoes in the microwave, 3 at a time. Cook on HIGH (100%) for 3 minutes. Place immediately in 425°F oven for 20 to 25 minutes or until done.

Feed the Kids

Golden Chicken Nuggets

1 pound boneless skinless chicken, cut into 1½-inch pieces

¼ cup *French's*® Sweet & Tangy Honey Mustard

2 cups *French's*® French Fried Onions, finely crushed

1. Preheat oven to 400°F. Toss chicken with mustard in medium bowl.

2. Place French Fried Onions into resealable plastic food storage bag. Toss chicken in onions, a few pieces at a time, pressing gently to adhere.

3. Place nuggets in shallow baking pan. Bake 15 minutes or until chicken is no longer pink in center. Serve with additional honey mustard.   *Makes 4 servings*

Prep Time: 5 minutes
Cook Time: 15 minutes

Chuckwagon BBQ Rice Round-Up

1 pound lean ground beef

1 (6.8-ounce) package RICE-A-RONI® Beef Flavor

2 tablespoons margarine or butter

2 cups frozen corn

½ cup prepared barbecue sauce

½ cup (2 ounces) shredded Cheddar cheese

1. In large skillet over medium-high heat, brown ground beef until well cooked. Remove from skillet; drain. Set aside.

2. In same skillet over medium heat, sauté rice-vermicelli mix with margarine until vermicelli is golden brown.

3. Slowly stir in 2½ cups water, corn and Special Seasonings; bring to a boil. Reduce heat to low. Cover; simmer 15 to 20 minutes or until rice is tender.

4. Stir in barbecue sauce and ground beef. Sprinkle with cheese. Cover; let stand 3 to 5 minutes or until cheese is melted.
                    Makes 4 servings

Tip: Salsa can be substituted for barbecue sauce.

Prep Time: 5 minutes
Cook Time: 25 minutes

Salsa Macaroni & Cheese

**1 jar (1 pound) RAGÚ® Cheese Creations!®
Double Cheddar Sauce**

1 cup prepared mild salsa

**8 ounces elbow macaroni, cooked and
drained**

1. In 2-quart saucepan, heat Ragú Cheese
Creations! Sauce over medium heat. Stir in
salsa; heat through.

2. Toss with hot macaroni. Serve immediately.
Makes 4 servings

Prep Time: 5 minutes
Cook Time: 15 minutes

Quick Tip

*To save time in preparing another meal, cook
twice as much pasta. Thoroughly drain pasta and
toss with oil. Cover and store in the refrigerator or
freezer. To reheat, rinse pasta in hot water or cook in
the microwave.*

Grilled Cheese & Turkey Shapes

8 slices seedless rye or sourdough bread

8 teaspoons *French's*® Mustard, any flavor

8 slices deli roast turkey

4 slices American cheese

**2 tablespoons butter or margarine,
softened**

1. Spread *1 teaspoon* mustard on each slice of
bread. Arrange turkey and cheese on half of
the bread slices, dividing evenly. Cover with
top halves of bread.

2. Cut out sandwich shapes using choice of
cookie cutters. Place cookie cutter on top of
sandwich; press down firmly. Remove excess
trimmings.

3. Spread butter on both sides of sandwich.
Heat large nonstick skillet over medium heat.
Cook sandwiches 1 minute per side or until
bread is golden and cheese melts.
Makes 4 sandwiches

Tip: Use 2½-inch star, heart, teddy bear or
flower-shaped cookie cutters.

Prep Time: 15 minutes
Cook Time: 2 minutes

Salsa Macaroni & Cheese

Feed the Kids

Corn Dogs

8 hot dogs

8 wooden craft sticks

1 package (about 16 ounces) refrigerated grand-size corn biscuits

⅓ cup *French's*® Classic Yellow® Mustard

8 slices American cheese, cut in half

1. Preheat oven to 350°F. Insert 1 wooden craft stick halfway into each hot dog; set aside.

2. Separate biscuits. On floured board, press or roll each biscuit into a 7×4-inch oval. Spread *2 teaspoons* mustard lengthwise down center of each biscuit. Top each with 2 pieces of cheese. Place hot dog in center of biscuit. Fold top of dough over end of hot dog. Fold sides towards center enclosing hot dog. Pinch edges to seal.

3. Place corn dogs, seam-side down, on greased baking sheet. Bake 20 to 25 minutes or until golden brown. Cool slightly before serving. *Makes 8 servings*

Tip: Corn dogs may be made without wooden craft sticks.

Prep Time: 15 minutes
Cook Time: 20 minutes

Ham & Cheese Shells & Trees

2 tablespoons margarine or butter

1 (6.2-ounce) package PASTA RONI® Shells & White Cheddar

2 cups fresh or frozen chopped broccoli

⅔ cup milk

1½ cups ham or cooked turkey, cut into thin strips (about 6 ounces)

1. In large saucepan, bring 2 cups water and margarine to a boil.

2. Stir in pasta. Reduce heat to medium. Gently boil, uncovered, 6 minutes, stirring occasionally. Stir in broccoli; return to a boil. Boil 6 to 8 minutes or until most of water is absorbed.

3. Stir in milk, ham and Special Seasonings. Return to a boil; boil 1 to 2 minutes or until pasta is tender. Let stand 5 minutes before serving. *Makes 4 servings*

Prep Time: 5 minutes
Cook Time: 20 minutes

Corn Dogs

Pizza Snack Cups

1 can (12 ounces) refrigerated biscuits (10 biscuits)

½ pound ground beef

1 jar (14 ounces) RAGÚ® Pizza Quick® Sauce

½ cup shredded mozzarella cheese (about 2 ounces)

1. Preheat oven to 375°F. In 12-cup muffin pan, evenly press each biscuit in bottom and up side of cups; chill until ready to fill.

2. In 10-inch skillet, brown ground beef over medium-high heat; drain. Stir in Ragú Pizza Quick Sauce and heat through.

3. Evenly spoon beef mixture into prepared muffin cups. Bake 15 minutes. Sprinkle with cheese and bake an additional 5 minutes or until cheese is melted and biscuits are golden. Let stand 5 minutes. Gently remove pizza cups from muffin pan and serve.

Makes 10 pizza cups

Prep Time: 10 minutes
Cook Time: 25 minutes

Quick Tip

For quick and easy clean up, serve pizza cups on napkins or paper towels.

Hot Diggity Dots & Twisters

⅔ cup milk

2 tablespoons margarine or butter

1 (4.8-ounce) package PASTA RONI® Four Cheese Flavor with Corkscrew Pasta

1½ cups frozen peas

4 hot dogs, cut into ½-inch pieces

2 teaspoons mustard

1. In large saucepan, bring 1¼ cups water, milk and margarine just to a boil.

2. Stir in pasta, peas and Special Seasonings; return to a boil. Reduce heat to medium. Gently boil uncovered, 7 to 8 minutes or until pasta is tender, stirring occasionally.

3. Stir in hot dogs and mustard. Let stand 3 to 5 minutes before serving.   *Makes 4 servings*

Prep Time: 5 minutes
Cook Time: 15 minutes

Quick Tip

To make kids' meals more fun, serve food on small colorful plates or fancy paper plates. Add finger foods like mini carrot sticks or apple slices for a complete nutritious meal.

Reese's® Haystacks

1⅔ cups (10-ounce package) REESE'S®
    Peanut Butter Chips

1 tablespoon shortening (do *not* use
    butter, margarine, spread or oil)

2½ cups (5-ounce can) chow mein noodles

1. Line tray with wax paper.

2. Place peanut butter chips and shortening in medium microwave-safe bowl. Microwave at HIGH (100%) 1 minute; stir. If necessary, microwave at HIGH an additional 15 seconds at a time, stirring after each heating, just until chips are melted and mixture is smooth when stirred. Immediately add chow mein noodles; stir to coat.

3. Drop mixture by heaping teaspoons onto prepared tray or into paper candy cups. Let stand until firm. If necessary, cover and refrigerate several minutes until firm. Store in tightly covered container.

Makes about 2 dozen treats

Quick Tip

Have kids help in preparing these snacks. They can increase math and reading skills while having fun preparing these simple delicious munchies.

Banana S'mores

1 firm DOLE® Banana, sliced

12 graham cracker squares

6 large marshmallows

1 bar (1.55 ounces) milk chocolate candy

Microwave Directions

• Arrange 4 banana slices on each of 6 graham cracker squares. Top with marshmallow. Microwave on HIGH 12 to 15 seconds or until puffed.

• Place 2 squares chocolate on remaining 6 graham crackers. Microwave on HIGH 1 minute or until just soft. Put halves together to make sandwich.   *Makes 6 servings*

Prep Time: 5 minutes
Cook Time: 1 minute

Feed the Kids

Brownie Peanut Butter Cupcakes

18 REYNOLDS® Foil Baking Cups

⅓ cup creamy peanut butter

¼ cup light cream cheese

2 tablespoons sugar

1 egg

1 package (about 19 ounces) fudge brownie mix

½ cup candy coated peanut butter candies

PREHEAT oven to 350°F. Place Reynolds Foil Baking Cups in muffin pans or on cookie sheet; set aside. Beat peanut butter, cream cheese, sugar and egg in bowl with electric mixer; set aside.

PREPARE brownie mix following package directions; set aside. Place 1 heaping teaspoon of peanut butter mixture in center of each baking cup. With spoon or small ice cream scoop, fill baking cups half full with brownie batter. Sprinkle each brownie cupcake with peanut butter candies.

BAKE 25 minutes; do not overbake. Cool.

Makes 18 brownie cupcakes

Scotcheroos

Nonstick cooking spray

1½ cups creamy peanut butter

1 cup granulated sugar

1 cup light corn syrup

6 cups toasted rice cereal

1⅔ cups (11-ounce package) NESTLÉ® TOLL HOUSE® Butterscotch Flavored Morsels

1 cup (6 ounces) NESTLÉ® TOLL HOUSE® Semi-Sweet Chocolate Morsels

COAT 13×9-inch baking pan with cooking spray.

COMBINE peanut butter, sugar and corn syrup in large saucepan. Cook over medium-low heat, stirring frequently, until melted. Remove from heat. Add cereal; stir until thoroughly coated. Press onto bottom of prepared baking pan.

MICROWAVE butterscotch morsels and semi-sweet chocolate morsels in large, microwave-safe bowl on HIGH (100%) power for 1 minute; stir. Microwave at additional 10- to 20-second intervals, stirring until smooth. Spread over cereal mixture.

REFRIGERATE for 15 to 20 minutes or until topping is firm. Cut into bars.

Makes 2½ dozen bars

Brownie Peanut Butter Cupcakes

Teddy Bear Party Mix

4 cups crisp cinnamon graham cereal

2 cups honey flavored teddy-shaped graham snacks

1 can (1½ ounces) *French's*® Potato Sticks

3 tablespoons melted unsalted butter

2 tablespoons *French's*® Worcestershire Sauce

1 tablespoon packed brown sugar

¼ teaspoon ground cinnamon

1 cup sweetened dried cranberries or raisins

½ cup chocolate, peanut butter or carob chips

1. Preheat oven to 350°F. Lightly spray jelly-roll pan with nonstick cooking spray. Combine cereal, graham snacks and potato sticks in large bowl.

2. Combine butter, Worcestershire, sugar and cinnamon in small bowl; toss with cereal mixture. Transfer to prepared pan. Bake 12 minutes. Cool completely.

3. Stir in dried cranberries and chips. Store in an air-tight container. *Makes about 7 cups*

Prep Time: 5 minutes
Cook Time: 12 minutes

Blue's Chillin' Banana Coolers

2 ripe medium bananas, peeled

4 flat wooden ice cream sticks

½ cup "M&M's"® Chocolate Mini Baking Bits

⅓ cup hot fudge ice cream topping, at room temperature

Line baking sheet with waxed paper; set aside. Cut each banana in half crosswise. Insert wooden stick about 1½ inches into center of cut end of each banana. Place on prepared baking sheet; freeze until firm, at least 2 hours. Place "M&M's"® Chocolate Mini Baking Bits in shallow dish. Place fudge sauce in separate shallow dish. Working with 1 banana at a time, place frozen banana in fudge sauce; turn banana and spread fudge sauce evenly onto banana with small rubber scraper. Immediately place banana on plate with "M&M's"® Chocolate Mini Baking Bits; turn to coat lightly. Return to baking sheet in freezer. Repeat with remaining bananas. Freeze until fudge sauce is very firm, at least 2 hours. Let stand 5 minutes before serving. Store tightly covered in freezer. *Makes 4 servings*

Hurry-Up Beverages

Orange Iced Tea

2 SUNKIST® oranges

4 cups boiling water

5 tea bags

Ice cubes

Honey or brown sugar to taste

With vegetable peeler, peel each orange in continuous spiral, removing only outer colored layer of peel (eat peeled fruit or save for other uses). In large pitcher, pour boiling water over tea bags and orange peel. Cover and steep 5 minutes. Remove tea bags; chill tea mixture with peel in covered container. To serve, remove peel and pour over ice cubes in tall glasses. Sweeten to taste with honey. Garnish with orange quarter-cartwheel slices and fresh mint leaves, if desired. *Makes 4 (8-ounce) servings*

Left to right: Orange Iced Tea and Lemon Herbal Iced Tea (page 182)

Mystic Chocolate Mint Cooler

2 cups cold whole milk or half-and-half

¼ cup HERSHEY'S Syrup

¼ cup white crème de menthe liqueur (mint-flavored liqueur)

1 cup crushed ice

Combine all ingredients except crushed ice in small pitcher; stir until well blended. Serve immediately over crushed ice.

Makes about 2 (10-ounce) servings

"A French" Banana Smoothie

2 (.53-ounce) envelopes SWISS MISS® Fat Free French Vanilla Cocoa Mix

½ cup fat free milk

½ ripe banana

1 tablespoon wheat germ (optional)

1 tablespoon honey (optional)

2 cups ice cubes

1. In blender, combine *all* ingredients.

2. Blend until thick and smooth.

Makes 2 (7-ounce) servings

Lemon Herbal Iced Tea

2 SUNKIST® lemons

4 cups boiling water

6 herbal tea bags (peppermint and spearmint blend or ginger-flavored)

Ice cubes

Honey or sugar to taste

With vegetable peeler, peel each lemon in continuous spiral, removing only outer colored layer of peel (save peeled fruit for other uses). In large pitcher, pour boiling water over tea bags and lemon peel. Cover and steep 10 minutes. Remove tea bags; chill tea mixture with peel in covered container. To serve, remove peel and pour over ice cubes in tall glasses. Sweeten to taste with honey. Garnish with lemon half-cartwheel slices, if desired. *Makes 4 (8-ounce) servings*

Swiss Berry Freeze

2 cups unsweetened frozen raspberries

2 cups fat free milk

2 (1¼-ounce) envelopes SWISS MISS® Premiere Chocolate Raspberry Truffle Cocoa Mix

Combine *all* ingredients in blender; blend until smooth. Add ice if desired; blend.

Makes 3 (9-ounce) servings

Chocoberry Refresher

1¼ cups cold 1% lowfat milk

1 container (8 ounces) vanilla lowfat
   yogurt

¼ cup HERSHEY'S Syrup

¼ cup HERSHEY'S Strawberry Syrup

Ice cubes (optional)

1. Place all ingredients except ice cubes in blender container. Cover; blend until smooth.

2. Pour into 3 glasses over ice cubes, if desired. Serve immediately.

Makes 3 (8-ounce) servings

Virgin Pineapple Colada

1 cup DOLE® Pineapple Juice

1 cup crushed ice

1½ tablespoons sugar

1 tablespoon lime juice

½ teaspoon coconut extract

Combine pineapple juice, ice, sugar, lime juice and extract in blender container. Cover; blend until thick and smooth. Garnish with lime peel, if desired. Serve immediately.

Makes 2 servings

Prep Time: 10 minutes

Peanut Butter Chocolate Twist Shake

6 ounces frozen vanilla yogurt or ice
   cream

4 ounces coconut juice or milk

1 ounce chocolate chips

1 ounce peanut butter

2 curls shaved chocolate

½ ounce crushed roasted peanuts

Whip all ingredients except shaved chocolate and peanuts together in blender until smooth. Garnish with shaved chocolate and crushed roasted peanuts.   *Makes 1 serving*

Favorite recipe from **Peanut Advisory Board**

Apple Smoothie

3 cups Michigan Apple cider or Michigan
   Apple juice

1 cup vanilla lowfat yogurt

1 package (3.4 ounces) instant vanilla
   pudding mix

Apple pie spice (optional)

In small bowl, combine Michigan Apple cider, yogurt and pudding mix. Whisk with wire whip until smooth. Refrigerate 2 hours before serving. Sprinkle with apple pie spice just before serving, if desired.   *Makes 4 servings*

Favorite recipe from **Michigan Apple Committee**

"M&M's"®
Brain Freezer Shake

2 cups any flavor ice cream

1 cup milk

¾ cup "M&M's"® Chocolate Mini Baking
  Bits, divided

Aerosol whipped topping

Additional "M&M's"® Chocolate Mini
  Baking Bits for garnish

In blender container combine ice cream and
milk; blend until smooth. Add ½ cup "M&M's"®
Chocolate Mini Baking Bits; blend just until
mixed. Pour into 2 glasses. Top each glass with
whipped topping; sprinkle with remaining
¼ cup "M&M's"® Chocolate Mini Baking Bits.
Serve immediately.

Makes 2 (1¼-cup) servings

Marshmallow
Chocolate Shake

2 cups fat free vanilla ice cream

¾ cup nonfat milk

⅓ cup SWISS MISS® Fat Free Hot Cocoa Mix
  with Mini Marshmallow

⅛ teaspoon almond extract (optional)

Combine *all* ingredients in blender; blend
until smooth.   *Makes 3 (6-ounce) servings*

Cranberry 'n' Lemon
Tea Punch

3 cups boiling water

6 tea bags

½ cup sugar

3 cups cranberry juice cocktail

¾ cup fresh squeezed lemon juice (juice of
  4 to 5 SUNKIST® lemons)

Ice cubes

In large pitcher, pour boiling water over tea
bags. Cover and steep 5 minutes. Remove tea
bags. Stir in sugar. Add cranberry and lemon
juices; chill. Serve over ice. Garnish with
lemon peel twists, if desired.

Makes 7 (8-ounce) servings

Iced French Roast

2 cups strong brewed French roast coffee,
  chilled

2 tablespoons low-fat milk

2 teaspoons sugar

½ teaspoon unsweetened cocoa powder

Dash ground cinnamon

Place all ingredients in blender; process until
combined. Pour over ice and serve immediately.

Makes 2 servings

Favorite recipe from **The Sugar Association, Inc.**

"M&M's"® Brain Freezer Shakes

Acknowledgments

The publisher would like to thank the companies and organizations listed below for the use of their recipes and photographs in this publication.

BC-USA, Inc.

BelGioioso® Cheese, Inc.

Birds Eye®

Bob Evans®

Butterball® Turkey

Cherry Marketing Institute

ConAgra Foods®

Del Monte Corporation

Dole Food Company, Inc.

Duncan Hines® and Moist Deluxe® are registered trademarks of Aurora Foods Inc.

Eagle Brand®

Filippo Berio® Olive Oil

Florida's Citrus Growers

The Golden Grain Company®

Guiltless Gourmet®

Hebrew National®

Heinz North America

Hershey Foods Corporation

The Hidden Valley® Food Products Company

Hillshire Farm®

Holland House® is a registered trademark of Mott's, Inc.

Keebler® Company

Lawry's® Foods

© Mars, Incorporated 2004

Michigan Apple Committee

National Pork Board

National Turkey Federation

Nestlé USA

Newman's Own, Inc.®

Peanut Advisory Board

Perdue Farms Incorporated

The Quaker® Oatmeal Kitchens

Reckitt Benckiser Inc.

Reynolds Consumer Products, A Business of Alcoa Inc.

Sargento® Foods Inc.

The J.M. Smucker Company

StarKist® Seafood Company

The Sugar Association, Inc.

Property of © 2003 Sunkist Growers, Inc. All rights reserved.

Unilever Bestfoods North America

Washington Apple Commission

Wisconsin Milk Marketing Board

METRIC CONVERSION CHART

VOLUME MEASUREMENTS (dry)

$1/8$ teaspoon = 0.5 mL
$1/4$ teaspoon = 1 mL
$1/2$ teaspoon = 2 mL
$3/4$ teaspoon = 4 mL
1 teaspoon = 5 mL
1 tablespoon = 15 mL
2 tablespoons = 30 mL
$1/4$ cup = 60 mL
$1/3$ cup = 75 mL
$1/2$ cup = 125 mL
$2/3$ cup = 150 mL
$3/4$ cup = 175 mL
1 cup = 250 mL
2 cups = 1 pint = 500 mL
3 cups = 750 mL
4 cups = 1 quart = 1 L

VOLUME MEASUREMENTS (fluid)

1 fluid ounce (2 tablespoons) = 30 mL
4 fluid ounces ($1/2$ cup) = 125 mL
8 fluid ounces (1 cup) = 250 mL
12 fluid ounces ($1\frac{1}{2}$ cups) = 375 mL
16 fluid ounces (2 cups) = 500 mL

WEIGHTS (mass)

$1/2$ ounce = 15 g
1 ounce = 30 g
3 ounces = 90 g
4 ounces = 120 g
8 ounces = 225 g
10 ounces = 285 g
12 ounces = 360 g
16 ounces = 1 pound = 450 g

DIMENSIONS

$1/16$ inch = 2 mm
$1/8$ inch = 3 mm
$1/4$ inch = 6 mm
$1/2$ inch = 1.5 cm
$3/4$ inch = 2 cm
1 inch = 2.5 cm

OVEN TEMPERATURES

250°F = 120°C
275°F = 140°C
300°F = 150°C
325°F = 160°C
350°F = 180°C
375°F = 190°C
400°F = 200°C
425°F = 220°C
450°F = 230°C

BAKING PAN SIZES

Utensil	Size in Inches/Quarts	Metric Volume	Size in Centimeters
Baking or Cake Pan (square or rectangular)	8×8×2	2 L	20×20×5
	9×9×2	2.5 L	23×23×5
	12×8×2	3 L	30×20×5
	13×9×2	3.5 L	33×23×5
Loaf Pan	8×4×3	1.5 L	20×10×7
	9×5×3	2 L	23×13×7
Round Layer Cake Pan	8×1½	1.2 L	20×4
	9×1½	1.5 L	23×4
Pie Plate	8×1¼	750 mL	20×3
	9×1¼	1 L	23×3
Baking Dish or Casserole	1 quart	1 L	—
	1½ quart	1.5 L	—
	2 quart	2 L	—